My Father's Servant Heart; Mi Padre, Su Amor

My Father's Servant Heart; Mi Padre, Su Amor

The Extraordinary Life of a Faithful Man

MARIA HENRIETTA MARTÍNEZ HUGHES

XULON PRESS

Xulon Press
2301 Lucien Way #415
Maitland, FL 32751
407.339.4217
www.xulonpress.com

Paperback ISBN-13: 978-1-6628-7392-8
Hard Cover ISBN-13: 978-1-6628-7393-5
Ebook ISBN-13: 978-1-6628-7394-2

Table of Contents

Dedication

For my sons, Lucas Daniel and Adam Steven; my husband Steve; and most of all for my dear Mother and Father in heaven.

A Note about this Book

What is described here is what I have tried to re-create from my memories. Although I have made every effort to ensure that the information in this book is correct, I have included my personal feelings, experiences, and emotions about our family. This is my story.

I hope you enjoy reading about my father, Ignacio, and my mother, Catalina, and their impact on our family, the parish, and the community.

Foreword

November 27, 2020

Ignacio Martínez will always be in my memory as a wonderful example of what a Deacon is all about. He lived an exemplary life as a faithful husband, devoted father, good neighbor, and dedicated servant. In many ways he was simple and never drew attention to himself. Yet the power of his attitudes and actions impacted many people and serve as an example of servant leadership.

Holiness is how I think of Ignacio. I was a young priest in the 70's just beginning my ministry when we met. I thank God for putting him in my life as a mentor and role model. He was what the Catholic diaconate was meant to be. He inspired my young priesthood and left me with memories and challenges that have lasted through my own retirement.

May his story and his goodness inspire your life as it certainly did mine!

Father David García
Former Pastor
Immaculate Conception Church
San Antonio, TX

Introduction

This story is about a man who persevered through his life's toughest challenges. It is my story about my father, Ignacio T. Martínez, who lived a life I am so proud to share. He was a Mexican American man born into a town, Sabinal, TX; where his ethnic background determined whether or not he received an education and job opportunities available to everyone else. He experienced bigotry starting at a young age and he knew that if he gave in to hate or resentment, he would be doomed for failure. He was determined to survive the bigotry and extreme poverty. His parents were extremely poor and had a large family to care for. Being Mexican American sealed their fate in Sabinal. The only opportunities available to them were field hand jobs and hard labor. The schools catered to the Anglo-Saxon families and the rich in this town. Even the cemeteries were separated by race and economic status. All through his formative years, my father prayed, struggled, and eventually made a life for himself and his family. All this was done with God's help and his undying faith in God's promises as described in the Gospels. He raised a family of ten children and educated them in Catholic schools at the objection of so many people who tried to discourage him from spending his money on private Catholic education. Our father knew educating his children in the Catholic faith was what God wanted. He had promised God that if he survived the Great Depression, bigotry, and illness, he would raise all his children in the Catholic faith. He kept his promise to God. God was right next to our father every step of the way through his 85 years of life.

Every single day since I can remember my father would say, "I owe so much to God that I spend my days doing all I can to help everyone that is suffering. I know I can never repay him, but I can try." His undying commitment towards helping others through spiritual and corporal works of mercy[1] is to be commended. He never wanted any recognition for any of his charitable work nor did he want recognition from the folks he was helping. He was just doing God's work as God was asking it of him. He never complained about the many interruptions that came his way by those who needed him. He was happy to serve and complete his mission as a servant of God.

This story describes how our father practiced the corporal and spiritual works of mercy in his daily life. He trusted God completely in every situation throughout his life, especially during the darkest times in his life. He knew God would not abandon him. He wanted very much to show his children by his actions that all gifts, whether spiritual or material, came from God. He wanted to teach his faith through his actions by living as God asks us to live. He loved his fellow man just as he loved himself. That is a true testament to his complete surrender to God. All through our lives we knew how special our father was. It was beautiful to see God's plan for his life unfold before our eyes. He always said that his faith began when he was a little boy. He wanted to become a priest, so when he was ordained a permanent Deacon on December 17, 1979; it was a true honor.

He suffered poverty and at several points illness almost killed him. He was left with weak lungs and was thin throughout his youth making him appear frail. He was denied entry into the military due to this illness that left him weak and vulnerable. However, his mind was bright and his will to succeed with God's help never wavered. He had a goal in mind to become

---

[1] The works of mercy are charitable actions by which we come to the aid of our neighbor in their spiritual and bodily necessities. Instructing, advising, consoling, comforting are spiritual works of mercy, as are forgiving and bearing wrongs patiently. The corporal works of mercy consist especially in feeding the hungry, sheltering the homeless, clothing the naked, visiting the sick and imprisoned, and burying the dead. Among all these, giving alms to the poor is one of the chief witnesses to fraternal charity: it is also a work of justice pleasing to God.

successful and to someday raise a family like the one he came from. His mother was extremely religious and always gave God thanks for her family's survival. The Great Depression was very hard on them and the bigotry they suffered made their life difficult. The church was the only place they could go to for comfort and donations to keep the family fed. Our father spoke of his mother on many occasions, and although she passed away before most of us were born, we knew she was a great influence on our father. He credited her for instilling in him his great faith in God. I find his life amazing not only because he was my father but because it's a story so full of sadness; yet happiness conquered because God had a plan for him. They accepted these challenges as "part of life." It was the way they handled these difficulties because of their faith in God that makes this story powerful and beautiful.

Chapter 1

Our Father Looked Forward to Death with Joy

~

Our father knew that if he passed away before our mother, we would care for her until her passing. This was a promise we made to our father almost on a daily basis for the last 10 years or so prior to his death. I think he knew that at their advanced age, he and our mother needed to prepare us for their eventual departure from this earth. Our father's passing came unexpectedly and his death left us in sorrow and shock. Our mother was under several doctors' care at that time and she seemed to be the one in danger of passing away first. Our fathers passing was probable but no one imagined it would be so sudden. Once he became very sick and the doctors could do no more, we accepted he was dying and we began to prepare for his death.

I imagined my father's last days would be very different than how they happened. I imagined we would all assist our mother as she cared for our father during his last days. I imagined we would all read to him during his last days from the beautiful gospels he spoke about every Sunday. Perhaps after that we would gather for a farewell Mass and say our goodbyes taking photos of our last days with him here on earth. God had other plans for him.

Our father prepared for his death every day of his life by living his life according to God's commandments. He loved life but as he aged, he spoke more and more about living in an eternal life just as God teaches. One of his favorite lines he recited was, "I am ready to go or I just want my "bell" to ring so I can join God for all of eternity." This made us sad but content that our father had such a great faith that he did not fear death; he looked forward to it.

God knew exactly when to take our father home. God's timing is always perfect. Our father's job of raising his ten children in the Catholic faith was completed and he was content that everyone was married and settled in their lives. He had the pleasure of baptizing some of his grandchildren and married some of his children while serving as a permanent Deacon at Immaculate Conception Church.

As soon as our father passed, I started to question my faith. I felt that God should have given us some indication our father's death was near. I was in shock and his death was absolutely unacceptable to me. His death was extremely agonizing for me personally. My mind went into a whirlwind trying to understand what was happening to our family.

I am a middle child and the eldest of the younger set of five children from a family of ten children. I am the one our father counted on for caring for the last four younger children through elementary, middle, and high school. Our five older siblings had moved on to Catholic high schools and colleges. So naturally, I was privileged to have lots of communication time with our father. We also became close after I suffered a major head injury in the eighth grade that required a miracle from God. This experience brought us closer together and he taught me how to pray in thanksgiving for God's healing.

Our mother, Catalina's, care was a priority in our lives after my father passed away. We did not know how this responsibility would affect the dynamics in our family or if our respective spouses would be supportive. While our parents had plenty of experience caring for others, we did not have experience with caregiving or medical care experience of any kind. We were unsure of what was coming or what was going to be required from us. It was our father's last request to care for our mother and without hesitation; we all gave him our promise. It was an agonizing time for all of us. The head of our family and our spiritual mentor had passed away. The grief was unbearable and time seemed to have stopped.

Faith was the only thing that gave us consolation. He lived a holy life, always working towards a happy death and most importantly wished to share eternity with God. God was pleased with his good and faithful servant. Letting go was difficult even if our father made it very clear to us that death was a joy. He looked forward to his death with great enthusiasm. God showed our father throughout his life how much he loved him by answering all our father's prayers especially in the most difficult times of his life.

We rejoiced in knowing our father was finally receiving his eternal reward from God. However, it was human nature to grieve for him and we found it difficult to accept his death. I was inconsolable and fell into a severe depression. This was my first encounter with a high level of anxiety and sadness. This condition affected my ability to think, to work, to proceed with my daily duties, or even show affection to my two sons. I felt like I was in a nightmare and I was never waking up.

There was no joy and this depression was debilitating. Medication helped me function with my daily activities. I spoke to my employer and received a three-month leave from my job in order to address the depression. Prayer was my only form of peace. My heart was broken, and it was hurting. I decided to start attending daily Mass knowing that God would help me accept our father's death. By receiving the Holy Eucharist every day, I began to feel some healing in my heart and eventually I began to accept his death as a reward for our father.

We anticipated that as our parents aged we would be required to make hard decisions regarding their care, but at this particular time that chore seemed far away. One is never prepared to bury a parent or anyone in their immediate family. Our father passed away during a very busy time in the church year; four days before the celebration of the birth of our Savior.

Archbishop Patrick Flores was a great friend to our father and visited him at the hospital. He suggested we say our goodbyes to our father and ask him to go to God. He reminded us that God was waiting for him and had prepared a place for our father. Therefore, we prayed the rosary as a family in his hospital room and then said our goodbyes.

It was a situation that I can honestly say was shocking to me and my family. We stayed in the hospital until the funeral home came for his body. The next morning, we began planning our father's funeral and began to accept the fact that he was not coming home ever again. Our mother did not sleep that night.

Our father fell ill on December 10, 2000, and eleven days later on December 21, he passed away to his eternal reward. The parish was shocked to hear of our father's passing since he was the one that had been organizing and preparing for the celebration of the birth of Jesus.

The program for his funeral Mass read, "Well done, good and faithful servant, enter into the joy of the master", Matthew 25:21.

One of our brothers, wrote the following and it was etched on his tombstone:

In loving memory of Deacon Ignacio T. Martinez
who devoted his life to the service of others.
His countless contributions to Immaculate Conception Parish will long
serve as testimony that he truly loved God above all else,
and that he loved his neighbor as himself.
May he rest in peace.

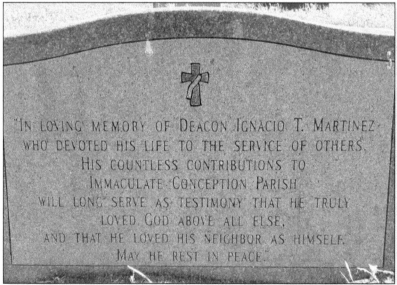

Archbishop Flores and Father Bill Collins, then Pastor of Immaculate Conception Church, decided to have the funeral as soon as possible due to the Christmas schedule. On December 22, 2000, our father's body entered

Immaculate Conception Catholic Church, a place where he served the people of God for 21 years as a Deacon. It was time to celebrate his life and to pray a Rosary to our Blessed Mother and for the repose of his soul. He looked as if he was just asleep. His illness was short and did not affect his appearance whatsoever. He looked very handsome in his suit and his ecclesiastical stole[2] placed across his chest. The church was full to capacity and people had standing room only. People paid their respects and walked in front of his casket for about two hours before the Rosary began. It was humbling to our mother and our family to see so many people accompanying us in our sorrow.

My older sister prepared and recited a beautiful tribute to our father. She spoke of our father's unending love for the poor and his tremendous trust in God. She spoke about the many relatives who stayed with us in our humble home all through the years. She called our front door, "a revolving door" where everyone and anyone who entered was greeted with love. Our parents were there to offer a kind word, a kind gesture or just peaceful conversation. Many times they would share a meal or coffee just to put everyone at ease so they could speak to our parents about their struggles or needs. I considered this normal, but now as an adult I know stopping everything at a moment's notice to help someone else (relative or not) is indeed a very kind Christian thing to do, and a sign of love; a corporal work of mercy.

She spoke of our father's plight with segregation and how he offered this experience to God for guidance and support. She spoke about his illnesses and how at least three times in his 85 years of life, he was close to an early death. During his illness when he could not work, he refused to remove his children from Catholic schools and instead pleaded to the schools to wait on payment. The highlight of her eulogy was about his undying love for God and Our Lady of Guadalupe. She spoke of his generous heart and

---

[2] Ecclesiastical Stole: Worn by Deacons in the Catholic Church

steadfast love for the Mass. There was no greater love our father had than for the Eucharist.

She made it clear that our father never boasted or spoke of the many good deeds he performed on behalf of God. Our father stated that a good deed does not need a thank you or a returned favor. He knew God was seeing and blessing all that we did in His name. Our father stressed that good deeds did not need an audience. She spoke of our father's God given gifts of compassion, empathy, love, and patience towards others. When pressed for answers of why he did so much for others, he stated, "That is our commandment from God, to love others as we love ourselves." She described some of the loving acts of service we witnessed our father performing through the years. He must have performed many more acts of charity but only God knew what those were.

Once, our father was asked to lead the City Council of San Antonio in prayer. At first, he did not consider himself worthy of such an honor. He thought that maybe a more educated and polished individual would best serve this role. However, after praying to God he found this an opportunity to share God's words of service and love to the people of San Antonio. His humility was evident when he spoke, and when finished he just walked away, not expecting any accolades from anyone. It was just how God created him, simple and loving.

In November of 2000, a month before my father passed, I was visiting him and he was watching a televised funeral for the beloved and long serving Congressman, Henry B. Gonzalez held at San Fernando Cathedral. While watching the funeral, he saw hundreds of people paying their respects. Our father made a comment, "It would be so amazing to have such a funeral when one dies." One month later at the same church, our father had as many if not more people honoring our father's life and work with the Catholic Church and the poor of this city. Archbishop Patrick Flores gave our father the same respect and honor at his funeral as he had to the Congressman in addition to honoring our father's work with the poor. Hundreds of people attended our father's funeral at San Fernando Cathedral. Politicians, attorneys, heads of companies, city council members, our co-workers, and parish friends were in attendance honoring our father. I do not know how many people attended but the Cathedral was full to capacity and had standing room only. It was a humbling experience for all of us and I am sure God was pleased.

I remember seeing a sea of black suits and some folks I knew who served the poor and homeless in San Antonio. Just to see such a love for our father by people we had never met made us very happy. If he were watching, I am sure he would have been astonished and said that he was just doing God's work. He may not have accomplished great things, but he achieved greatness by responding to the simple call to service and faithfulness to God. He endured poverty and persevered over medical challenges yet despite these struggles he never lost hope. We were extremely grateful to everyone who joined us in the celebration of our father's life and his passage to his heavenly reward.

We wanted to take down all the Christmas decorations from our mother's tree but she would not allow us to remove anything just yet. We felt an intense sadness and the last thing we wanted to see was Christmas decorations. She kept repeating how much our father liked this time of the year and leaving the tree up for a while gave her some comfort. To understand our father's family dynamics, one would have to place oneself in our father's shoes beginning in his early teen years. He consecrated[3] himself and his family to God every day and this book will help explain why he dedicated his life to assisting the poor and the needy. Understanding his life as a young Mexican-American teen in a segregated small town, namely Sabinal, TX, and his difficulties reveals how he built a foundation of total trust in God and his strong steadfast faith in God's promises.

---

[3] Consecrated himself to God: He wanted everything that he did to honor God or be part of God's plan for him.

Chapter 2

Learning to Live without my Father

⟵ᵔ

My father's death was a very difficult time for me personally. He was my confidant, my advisor, my mentor, and my spiritual director. I loved my father so much and we had a very strong bond. One time when I was in eighth grade, a student at our school was swinging an iron milk crate and lost control of it. As soon as he let go of the crate it came flying directly into the right side of my head. I was standing on the pitcher's mound when the crate flew into my head. The force of the iron crate knocked me unconscious and dragged me on my face across the grass. It took the school two hours before they called my father. The nuns began to see that I was not speaking properly and I kept repeating myself. They saw I had temporary memory loss and it frightened them. My face was beginning to swell and they became very concerned. I do not know if they knew what to do other than to call my father.

The author and 3 of her siblings ready for school at Immaculate
Conception Parish School in the 1960s.

According to my father, God performed a miracle that day for him and
me. I did not suffer a loss of IQ or any permanent memory loss as head injuries can cause at times. As my father walked into the hallway at the school
and our eyes met, my memory returned and I ran to hug him. He told me
that on his way to the school he prayed every prayer he could remember
and asked God to save me from brain injury or worse, an early death. He
relayed this story to me many times over telling me God had saved my life
that day. I think the school thought our father was going to sue them or bill
them for medical costs. Our parents did nothing of the sort. Instead, they
prayed with me every day thanking God that I was alive and would soon
be back to normal. I looked like a monster with swelling on both sides of
my face and had a couple of black eyes, so I missed quite a bit of school. My
father had a very calming way about him and he made sure I did not worry

about my face. He made sure my younger sister brought my homework to me every day. He was a very gentle person and I feel very fortunate God picked him as my father. God blessed us greatly with such a faithful man who constantly instilled in us the love of God.

For that reason, I became very close with my father and listened intently to every word when he spoke, especially when he mentioned his mission of helping the poor. The twinkle in his eye when he spoke of God's love stayed forever in my mind's eye. I loved it when he dismissed us with the words, "I am praying for you". He spoke to us frequently about the fullness of spiritual grace[4] for our everyday life and he expressed how blessed he had been because God kept His promises. He wrote his sermons and his eulogies for funerals at his desk that was located at the entrance of our home. I have vivid images of him sitting at his desk reading and typing his sermons with such passion and love. If our children would interrupt him while he was writing, he would stop, greet them with a hug, and listen intently to whatever they had to say. He would always give them words of encouragement and love; a spiritual work of mercy, no doubt.

He was an instructor of baptism, preparations for marriage, and most importantly, he was a catechist to the youth of the parish. He enjoyed ministering to the young because he could share his story with them motivating them to trust God in all things. As a matter of fact, the young families that attended our father's funeral services spoke to us about the baptisms and funerals our father had presided over. They expressed their love for his sensitivity, his spirituality, and the many words of guidance he gave them asking them to live a Holy life.

Most remembered were his words of encouragement to those suffering economic and emotional stress, advising them to make Mass an everyday habit. Telling them that God keeps His promises to us; we just have to ask Him. Our father was not trying to save the world, he was living his life as

---

[4] Spiritual Grace: He believed that grace he received was a gift from God that helped with his ministry and everyday life.

God taught us. His passion and love for the Mass made his life of service a great joy. He was a very humble man, and if he had heard these tributes from the parishioners he would have excused them as nothing but God's work. Hearing these people speak of our father sounded almost like they were speaking about a saint, not our father, yet we knew we too had experienced the same invitation from our father to love and trust God.

As a family, we realized we needed to begin having family meetings in order to discuss our mother's care. Her medication list was numerous and one of father's last requests as he entered the operating room was to pay attention to her medications. One of his last requests was to have one of my younger sisters directly care for my mother and her medications. We needed to become familiar with all her physicians. Did the insurance cover caregivers and should we hire someone to cover when we were not available? Questions seemed to be coming out of nowhere from all of us. It was confusing and exhausting as we discussed the different scenarios of what could go wrong. One of our brothers, José Rafael, was a firefighter so he researched the information medical technicians would need in the event of an emergency and took the lead by preparing her home for such an event.

Our mother insisted on being present in all our meetings; however, she was not able to remember the particulars of her medical conditions. I believe it was her way of showing us that she did not want to be left alone. We needed God to guide us and help us become what our mother and father expected of us. We immersed ourselves in prayer and at the same time experienced such sadness missing our father. We gathered as often as possible and decided email was the only form of communication that appealed and worked for everyone. Email between all ten of us ensured that important information affecting our mother reached everyone immediately.

Another of our brothers, Telesforo Simon, who resembles our father very much, was the executor of our father's will and he took the lead in setting up our family meetings. Our father had sat with him on many occasions preparing him for this day when he would be gone and we would be left behind to care for our mom.

Our mother was not familiar with her medications or her doctor's names. She was dependent on our father for that information. He kept her doctors' appointment schedule and her medications organized. Immediately after our father's burial, she became extremely quiet and retreated into her own world. She was deeply confused and in a state of shock, like us. This was so unexpected that our minds were still in denial of his death. Our father's concern regarding her memory loss was something he shared with us in our daily conversations with him. He knew her memory was deteriorating, and he feared her condition would only worsen as she aged. At this particular time; we did not know how severe our mother's dementia was or how it was affecting her daily life. We did not seem to agree on much anyway, we were in a state of bewilderment and sadness. It was obvious some of us had a greater influence on our mother than others. This created some division and tension between us.

There was only one thing we all agreed on and that was to care for our mother to the very best of our ability. We knew we needed a plan, and building that plan was time consuming and urgent at the same time. Ten siblings in one room all thinking we would figure it all out in one day was unrealistic, but we tried. We began every conversation with prayer. Our goal was to keep things as normal as possible in our mother's life. Asking her to move in with one of us was neither our father's wish nor hers, so that was not a consideration. She liked being in her familiar surroundings and her neighbors were kind people she had known for a long time.

There is a heavy sadness when a person loses a spouse of 60 years that I imagine is devastating. What I did see in our mother was deep grief that no one could temper or take away. She had always been the "non-crying" type of woman, always positive, strong, persevering, and courageous, and here she was lost. I cried just watching her stoic facial expression; the face you see of a person who has given up on life. We continued attending Mass at their parish and not seeing our father at the altar brought tears to our eyes; however, our mother stayed motionless. God knew how much our parents had shared, prayed, and encouraged each other. God knew it was time to start preparing her for her eternal reward. She became anxious and at times she was lucid. She would talk about our father but it would not last very long. We knew she understood he had passed away, but I think she dreamt of him and that alone confused her. As for me personally, I had to reestablish my relationship with our mother again, not as a person for me to lean on, but as a person who had medical, emotional, and physical needs. It was faith alone that enabled us to keep our mother in her home until her passing. At this point, I was falling in love with my mother all over again and accepted that she needed me, needed us, needed her family more than ever before. Well, there were ten of us; surely this would be easy. However, it was not as easy as we thought.

We could not allow our mother to live alone due to her many illnesses but more importantly because of her dementia. Her advanced dementia and her grieving handicapped her so much that at times she retreated to silence. It was indeed a sad and helpless situation for her, and we felt sympathy and love for her. God was with us and we knew He would not abandon her or us. She could not tell the daytime from the nighttime because she was not sleeping normally, and her health began to fail her almost immediately after our father's death. This was a helpless feeling for all of us. She became dependent on her children, and we became the parents. Two months after our father passed, our mother had a very dangerous medical condition surface, rectal prolapse. This condition only worsened over the next few months resulting in three surgeries before her death a few years later.

Chapter 3

Mom and Dad at the Beginning of their Life Together

Catalina and Ignacio were married in Sabinal on April 28, 1940.

God blessed our parents with a family of twelve children, eight girls and four boys. Two children passed away as infants due to different circumstances. As our family grew, they greeted each child with love and gratitude to God. Being Catholic and accepting children lovingly from God was all our parents wanted. Our parents' oldest child, Rosario, died from an unknown childhood illness. Our parents mentioned how polio and tuberculosis were killing people during the 1940's. She passed away in our mother's arms at the hospital. The emotional toll it took on both of them must have been devastating for such a young couple. They felt this tragedy with much sadness. A nurse at the hospital comforted our mother by telling her God would bless them again with many children. Our mother was not hearing anything; she was in much despair and sadness. Our father saw it another way, he felt God had spared this baby the purgatory of life and decided to take her straight to heaven. He never questioned death or why it happened. He knew God had His reasons and that was enough for our father.

Our parents named her Rosario, the Spanish word for Rosary. One of our nieces, who met Pope John Paul II, carries the name Rosario after her aunt. Our niece was born with a heart defect and shortly after birth, doctors operated on her tiny heart. My brother, Telesforo Simon is her father. His parish needed a representative to greet our Holy Father, so the priest suggested to Telesforo that if his little girl lived through the heart issue, she would be the one to greet the Holy Father. God healed her. She and our Telesforo greeted Pope John Paul II when he came to San Antonio along with other individuals chosen by the Archdiocese. The beautiful part of this story is that this experience elated our father and mother. Telesforo looks like a younger version of our father. He also bears the name of one of our uncles who our father loved as a son. That uncle, also named Telesforo Simon, our dad's younger brother, was a prisoner of war in Korea and when he was released he came to live with our family.

Praying the Rosary was our parents' nightly ritual and they shared it every night until the death of our father. When we were younger, our father would pace our sidewalk that led to our front door for a couple of hours to do his walking while praying the Rosary continuously. A few weeks after our father's passing a neighbor of theirs shared a story with us. She stated that when she moved next door and saw our father pacing the sidewalk and praying every night, she immediately thought that surely this man must have huge problems since he prayed every night for so long. This made our mother chuckle.

Ignacio holding their first born daughter Rosario in Sabinal in 1942.

Our sister, Rosario, is buried at the cemetery designated for Mexican Americans in Sabinal, where our parents met and married. Our father used to say, even in death Mexican Americans had to be segregated. He would say that this was against God's will. This town was embroiled by bigotry and extreme poverty. Our father and mother revealed to us that they felt as if God was punishing them in some way by taking their first-born baby. They knew they had their marriage blessed in the Catholic Church and their parish priest asked them to trust in God's mercy. These tough years were painful. However; little did they know that God was about to bless them abundantly.

Our father would encourage our mother to be in prayer and have faith in God. He believed God had a plan for them. These stories often made me wonder if our father was a mystic like St. Ignatius of Antioch[5]. My father always spoke with such confidence in God almost as if God himself revealed His words to our father in a face-to-face conversation. He was a great example of complete and total surrender to God.

Just as the hospital nurse had predicted, our parents began to have children a few years after their first child had passed away. They were elated and received every child with great joy and gratitude. Our father loved children as much as our mother and he felt extremely blessed by God. He shared with us that he would promise God a life of service upon the birth of every child. He knew the Holy Spirit would guide him and our mother in raising their large family. More than anything, he wished to provide his children with a Catholic school education. He believed whole-heartedly that this education would arm us with the faith we needed to face life's challenges.

During the 1940s, discrimination towards Mexican Americans was rampant in Sabinal. I recently saw the 1956 movie, "Giant," which portrays the unjust manner in which Mexican Americans were treated in small towns like this one, the reality was much worse. Our father was a very smart and handsome young man. He had a gentle looking face and was shy but friendly. He stood 5'9 and had a thin build. He revealed to us that he was one of the most intelligent students in his eighth-grade class. Our father's grandfather worked in a library and exposed my father to books constantly.

---

[5] Mystics of the Catholic Church: St. Ignatius of Antioch was an early Christian writer, martyr and bishop of Antioch. While en route to Rome, where he met his martyrdom, Ignatius wrote a series of letters. This correspondence now forms a central part of a later collection of works known to be authored by the Apostolic Fathers.

Our father loved to learn and he read every day. His personal library had so many interesting books including books on the lives of saints and other non-religious books. He loved his Catholic faith and his priest friends gave him books on special occasions like his birthday. Whenever he came across an article regarding the education of families in Catholic schools, he would stop and share them with us. Those articles gave him great hope that his and our mother's financial sacrifice of sending us to Catholic school was on track.

The school district in this segregated town did not allow Mexican Americans into high school. The superintendent of the school district and the teachers at the school knew our father had promise. They pleaded to the school board to make an exception for our father. The decision rendered was final and there was no appeal process, he could not attend high school. The school board was not interested in a Mexican American student furthering his education. This experience was a major disappointment to our father. However, God had other plans for him. He left school reluctantly but did not give up on learning or educating himself. The only option left for him now was working in the cotton fields. This type of hard labor demanded long hours in the hot sun and the job paid very little for such hard work. He needed God to help him discern what he would do next to escape this difficult and dangerous work in the cotton fields.

Our father knew he did not belong in the cotton fields and he longed for an education, a better life, and a place where he could raise a family. He longed for a career and a decent way of life. His faith is the only thing he could rely on. He knew his mother's devotion to God's promises was powerful. Only God would show him his way and only God could change this situation. He prayed every day at Mass and asked God to show him a way out of poverty and into a life of education and decent employment.

Our father's denial of getting a high school education was foremost on his mind and he was determined to remedy that injustice. He knew he was the smartest student in his class and he deserved an education like everyone else in his school. This experience became the catalyst that catapulted him towards planning a new life in a new city, perhaps San Antonio, TX. While at Mass, he asked God to guide him in a plan for the future. He asked God to remove the hatred and disdain he had for the people who robbed him of an education. He did not want to carry bitterness in his heart for it would surely rob him of a happy life. He knew God would not agree with hate and resentment. That attitude of forgiveness and love for his fellow man lasted until the day he passed away. He was a wonderful person with a gentle smile. He was a loving, caring, sensitive, and patient person who loved God above all else.

He was a very devout Catholic who knew his faith in God was all he needed to succeed. He believed in Divine intervention and saw how the understanding of a higher power was denied to some educated men. Faith was a gift and grace was abundant in his soul to forgive what segregation had done to him. Salvation was in the cross of Christ and that is why he started every day with 6:00 am Mass since the age of 11 years until his death at 85 years of age.

From time to time, he would revisit those difficult times reminding us how blessed we were to have all the opportunities of a Catholic education. He worked hard so we would not have to endure a life without a Catholic education and endure poverty as he once had. As a child, I did not fully understand his plight with discrimination or his personal story, but I knew our education was extremely important to him. Our father gave us one task and that was to study hard and make the grades. Our father turned to God for strength and guidance and passed that love of God to us. He knew that God had made his dreams possible and he felt indebted to God forever. He knew harboring resentment meant he was not fully surrendering to God's will. I have witnessed that most of us find forgiving people who hurt us nearly impossible. Our father did it anyway; he knew it would please God.

He was determined to do God's will without question or hesitation. This gift of faith leading to a life of grace and total surrender to God began at a very young age. Sometimes I wonder if he received Signal Grace[6] from God as a young child in order to forge forward after the difficulties he was going to face. My father was so distinctive in his service to God that our neighbors would often comment how much our father impressed them with his love of daily Mass. One neighbor thought he had been a priest at one time. He lived a very prayerful life. As a parent of adult children, I now understand why he prayed morning, noon, and night. He knew that if God sent him children surely God was asking him to guide them in the Catholic faith. He did not force or demand anything from us regarding our Mass attendance. He just showed us the love of Mass with his actions. He was a leader of a Men's Group early into his marriage to our mother and he enjoyed seeing these leaders of families committed to their faith in God.

Our father came from a family of eleven. The family consisted of five girls and six boys. He shared with us that our grandparents were devout Catholics. He always emphasized his great love towards his mother whom he called God's servant. Our father was an altar boy as a young boy and walked to church to serve Mass almost every day. He was only 10 years old and at such a young age he was already devoting himself to God. Our father revealed to us that they prayed as a family and these same prayers served as comfort during the very hard economic times.

The Great Depression of the 1930's brought immense poverty and disillusion to folks like my grandparents and parents. The Great Depression created a mindset that our parents never seemed to change. Our father always managed to save a little money for a rainy day. It was not much but he felt it was important to establish a savings because the economy was ever changing. The Great Depression left many families devastated and some never recovered. Our father would recount how some families had to live with extended relatives just to have food or a place to lay their heads.

Those stories would resonate in his actions for the rest of his life.

---

[6] Signal Grace: Signal graces are extraordinary graces that move the soul by the intellect and will in such a way that the reception of the grace can be seen by others.

Chapter 4

Struggles and Challenges

I do not remember our father or mother ever throwing anything away that was reusable. They always seemed to find someone who was in need and managed to get those items to them. Everything was recycled or handed down to the next child or passed on to a family in need. If we had an abundance of a particular food or vegetable, our mother would share with neighbors and with her sisters (and our cousins) who lived nearby.

A few years after we moved into our own home, our parents built a storage shed/shop to move our father's shop home after retirement, but also to store our belongings until a new owner was found. Our mother would enjoy sorting clothes, shoes, curtains, tools, and other items in that storage shed. It was nice to see her busy with organizing as a pastime for her and to see old furniture or mementos she had kept from days gone by. She kept everything to a fault; not like a hoarder but as a "just in case" someone might have a need. We managed to find items our families needed from tools to miscellaneous items we could use at our homes. All our report cards, First Communion certificates, hospital certificates, baptismal gowns, nursery bracelets we wore, and old porcelain dolls were a part of these great finds. Since our father's business occupied the front room of the shed, her items were in the second room of the shed. It was well built with a nice roof and had a small window air conditioning unit for the hot summer days. My aunt's son, Johnny, built the shed for my parents.

Our uncles joined the military and three of our aunts joined a religious community and became nuns. It appeared that everyone was escaping Sabinal due to a lack of educational opportunities for Mexican Americans. His other two sisters married, and raised families and moved away as well. Our father did not pass the required health screening so he did not qualify to serve in the military. He had a thin build and was underweight due to some health issues he endured as a child. Our grandfather advised him to finish his education since his thin frail body was not strong enough for hard labor. Our father was familiar with hard labor. He had once joined his friends picking cotton in the hot Texas sun because there were no other jobs available after he was forced to leave school.

Our father knew that if he stayed in the fields working, his health would be in peril. He yearned to continue an education and to build a career that would help him escape segregation. He was destined for a life of service and God was leading him to where He wanted him to be. He was not fearful of his future as long as he attended daily Mass and received the Holy Eucharist. He was a man of great dedication to his faith and he had a strong devotion to Adoration[7] as well. He attended Adoration every first Friday of the month. This practice lasted until his death in 2000. He also attended the Stations of the Cross[8] on Friday evenings during every Lent until his death. He loved being in close proximity to God and enjoyed spreading as much joy about our salvation as possible. The passion for his faith was obvious in seeing his "holiness" while he served at Mass with the priest. He served Mass with much devotion and love of God.

---

[7] Adoration: Catholic devotion to spend time praying and in adoration with the Body of Christ at a church.

[8] Stations of the Cross: Catholic devotion to prayer remembering the path that Jesus took to Calvary, known as the Via Dolorosa. Many churches hold these devotions on Fridays during the Lenten Season.

Our grandfather admired our father's great mind and advised him to work in a job that required "mental work." It was as if our grandfather had a premonition of things to come. He had complete faith in our father's abilities to continue studying and he knew our father had promise. God kept His promises of seeing our father through this complicated and hard time in his life. Our father had more of an engineering mind and did not have the personality to sell as his father did. His father sold vegetables in the streets of Sabinal for a living, and he enjoyed talking to people. Our father was shy and reserved but had a humorous side too.

Our father enjoyed quiet reading instead of the demanding sales job his father had. It was amusing to see our father ordained a Permanent Deacon in his later years because it required him to speak during homilies, funerals, baptisms, and during his service to the poor. I know the Holy Spirit gave him the courage to speak publicly and gave our father words of wisdom for his homilies. This story reminds me of Moses' encounter with God in the Book of Exodus, regarding his fear of speaking in which God tells Moses He will give him the words to speak. I now realize that our father's entire life was in preparation for becoming a servant of God. All of his trials and tribulations during his young years served him well in his ministry as a Permanent Deacon. His personal struggles sustained sensitivity to others and created a compassionate demeanor. He was extremely approachable, non-threatening, and very good with people in need. He was truly a servant of God serving God's people in every way he could. This was his life's mission and he loved it.

When he was already a Deacon preaching at a Mass in the 1980s at ICC.

Our grandmother was faithful to her prayer time and she shared her love of God openly with her family. She attended Mass every day. She raised her children in extreme poverty in a bigoted town yet managed to create children that loved God above all. Our father credited her constant praying to their strong wills in seeking a better life. He would often say to us, "my mother was a saint." He learned to pray from her great example as a devout Catholic. She recognized that their very survival depended on God's love and mercy.

Prayer kept his family close and sustained their dreams of escaping their impoverished situation. This family had endured sickness, poverty, discrimination, and a lack of education. Yet, out of this large family of eleven children, God called three siblings to serve as religious nuns and they responded with love and enthusiasm.God calls us to Himself no matter what is going on in our lives. "With God all things are possible" was one of our father's favorite sayings. His family lacked material things but were rich in faith and love. God was the focal point in their lives. Their faith was solid and our father stated that God never forgot them. They found joy in all things, especially in having a healthy family and surviving the Great Depression.

Our father's oldest sibling, Lilia, became a nun and joined an order, the Teresians, that required a monetary donation from the candidates' family. Our grandparents did not have any money so our father credits God for allowing our aunt to become a servant of God without the required monetary donations. Many others in her order came from very wealthy families and these donations helped sustain the needs of the order. Our father considered her acceptance into the religious order a miracle. He stated that his three sisters joining the convent solidified his parents' arrival into heaven. What a beautiful sentiment to share with us. I am sure our grandparents were very proud of all three of their daughters for choosing to dedicate their lives for God's work.

Catalina and Ignacio with Sr. Lilia at St Teresa Academy in 1967.

One of our aunts managed a retirement home in San Antonio (Padua Place) for priests that provided nursing and medical care. She worked there until her death in November of 2018. Our other aunt was a missionary and is currently retired. She worked by helping a parish located near her convent. Both aunts worked into their 90s doing God's work. The eldest of our aunts, Sr. Lilia, passed away at 100 years of age in December 2004. The nuns told us that for a few years before she passed, she would constantly bless herself with the sign of the cross. We witnessed her doing this shortly before she passed away.

The Holy Spirit[9] provided our father with gifts of counseling, optimism, stamina, and love for all of God's people. He always knew what to say to us when presented with a problem. He requested we pray and offer our trials to God in sacrifice. We never left his home or his presence without his promise to pray for us. What a beautiful sentiment for us, his children. His one famous line, "Be a good Christian" rings in my mind every day and I find myself looking for ways to do just that. Every effort I make today to be a "good Christian" is because our father taught me that living God's way has many rewards. He was a testament to that by the way he chose to live his life and later by receiving God's rewards.

Our father met our mother at a public function. Our mother's parents had passed away before she met our father. Her father passed away in Mexico and her mother died in a car accident here in the United States. Our mother's older sisters had married and lived wherever their husbands could find employment. Times were hard for Mexican Americans who were uneducated and unskilled. Some of these jobs were long distances away, so our aunts had to pick up and move their families as a matter of necessity. I believe most of the jobs available to Mexican Americans were jobs as ranch hands on large ranches or as migrant farm workers.

---

[9] Holy Spirit: According to sacred tradition the seven gifts of the Holy Spirit are wisdom, understanding, counsel, fortitude, knowledge, piety and awe or fear of the Lord.

During harvest time they would temporarily make their homes at the locations where they were working in the fields. This life was not an easy life for them. At times, only the men would leave to work on large farms in other states that were located as far away as Michigan. Our aunts would learn to be alone for long periods of time managing the best they could and raising their children alone. This is where our Catholic church has done such a wonderful job of educating our children, through private schools or catechism classes, before or after Mass. Our aunts devoted themselves to raising their children in the Catholic Church. The church often helped our aunts with food and other supplies.

Chapter 5

Our Mother and their Marriage

~~~~~~

Our mother embraced her Catholic faith and soon her sisters followed her and my father's example by devoting themselves to God and attending Mass. They entrusted their lives to God and began seeking a better life through prayer and sacrifice. Since they did not have telephones, they would write letters to each other. One of our aunts wrote to her older sibling informing her of our grandmother's passing. Upon reading of her mother's passing, our aunt fainted at the post office. I imagine this is what poor people experience when there is no other form of communication. These family disconnections due to economic struggles are so painful to hear about in this age of technology we live in today.

Our mother and her sisters were uneducated, and they had no one to protect them. Our mother explained that some folks spoke rudely about her and her sisters and of their lack of proper upbringing as women. This inferior feeling stayed with our mother for many years until she received an honor as Mother of the Year in 1983 from the city of San Antonio. The Express News had many categories in which they honored women; she was chosen in the Homemaking category. I nominated her for this honor because I felt she was a true example of a dedicated parent who worked tirelessly helping others. She was determined to be the best wife and mother and to raise her children as educated Catholic adults. She would always remind us how important it was to be an educated woman who could support a family and who could realize her full potential. She spoke of the importance of being independent and would often share her struggles as a mother and wife. These struggles pushed her to work harder and to trust God in all things. Like our father, her experiences as a child and young adult made her a valuable Christian woman with much to share. Her empathy for other wives and mothers who were suffering in poverty was tremendous. She would always shine a light on them with her advice of prayer and perseverance.

Our mother developed a thick skin for criticism and always conducted herself with respect and kindness. She earned acceptance by everyone she met simply by practicing her Catholic faith and showing kindness to everyone she met. She was an intelligent woman who had a knack for organization. She revealed to us that she always wanted to be a good parent and missed having her own mother to guide her. She was a beauty with fair skin, dark hair, light brown eyes, and a thin build. She had an infectious smile and a hearty laugh. She loved to say funny things. I remember her whistling in the kitchen as she prepared dinner. Those were happy times for me as a child watching her be so joyful.

Our parents married in a small Catholic church in Sabinal and family helped celebrate with a small celebration. Our father expressed his desire to move to a large city where segregation was not so prevalent. He wanted to ensure that his children would not face discrimination of any sort or lose an education because of their ethnicity. After a couple of years of marriage, our parents moved to Hondo, TX, where our father found employment. Our father worked at the Hondo Navigation School as a radio technician for airplanes and other government equipment. Later, he heard from his friends and family that San Antonio was a city of opportunity.

So, in 1945 he and our mother moved to San Antonio. Our father shared with us his story of complete surrender to God's will in all things. He prayed for guidance and grace to build a new life in a place where his children would thrive. It was when our mother agreed to move that he realized God had answered his prayers by motivating her to move to San Antonio. He needed her complete agreement in order for this to happen. She left her family behind and supported her husband. It was the best decision they ever made. Soon other family members followed them to San Antonio to begin a new life. God's plan was beginning to unfold.

I always enjoyed hearing this story as he told it. He always had a smile on his face when he looked back at this very important decision of moving to a larger city. The death of their first-born was always on their mind, and they felt that medical emergencies like the one they experienced with their baby would not be a problem in a city like San Antonio. He credited God with helping them during the most difficult situations he and our mother faced. He stated that he still had problems like any family but his faith made them less of a burden and somehow a solution always came through, namely a miracle. There is no one that I know like my father, who possesses so much fire in his eyes when he spoke about God's miracles. It was easy to see the passionate love for his faith as he spoke about God's many interventions in his life. I suppose unknowingly, he was our spiritual director who guided our faith throughout our lives.

They moved to San Antonio and our father began working with a radio and TV repair shop. He applied at Kelly Air Force base and began working once again in civil service as a radio technician. Later, he accepted a supervisor position as a promotion. He experienced the immense stress associated with being a middle management supervisor. He shared with us that workers would not show up for work after being off for the weekend. Our father was a very conscientious person so; this bothered him a great deal and he knew production was his responsibility. This left our father with extra work and added timeline pressures. The worry of meeting deadlines when workers did not show up for the assembly line and having the responsibility of a growing family was a lot to endure. Our father prayed for a divine inspiration for a solution. A way out of this "pressure cooker" job and a way to earn a living for his family who he desperately wanted to educate in the Catholic faith. Then another emergency occurred, but this time it was very personal. Our grandfather was dying and was in need of full-time care.

Our grandfather became ill with stomach cancer and our father brought him to San Antonio to live with us. He did not have anyone to care for him in Sabinal where he lived, and the medical care he needed also was not available. Our mother volunteered to care for our grandfather after our father's siblings were not able to help. Our mother's God given gifts of caregiving and love were very evident in this situation. Our father saw caring for his father as a calling from God. He knew he had a debt to pay and so he considered the opportunity to care for his father a privilege and an honor. Our father never discussed financial hardships due to our grandfathers care, but I am sure they existed. I am not aware of any Medicare, Medicaid, or any other government assistance that helped our parents with his care.

Our mother was pregnant with me during this time. It was 1955 and she was having their sixth child, yet she and our father accepted this duty with love and happiness. This had to be one of the most stressful times in their lives because the small house they rented had limited space. They could not remember how they fit another person in that duplex. I now understand why so many of our relatives have great respect for our parents. They did things others would not regardless of the sacrifices that they personally had to make. Those are the rules to live by according to what Jesus teaches. They were faithful servants who understood what love is and what faith can do. Fear was not a word in their vocabulary. They faced every challenge with complete confidence in God's help.

Our father wanted to be available in the event our grandfather or mother needed him. He knew his civil service job was not going to allow him to come home in the event of an emergency. His job had deadlines that were impossible to meet and those were important. His family was a priority in his life, and he prayed for guidance and inspiration to remedy this problem. He placed complete trust in God in this decision. He began taking TV and radio repair correspondence classes for $8.00 a month, and in 1955 he earned a certificate of completion for his studies in TV and repair service and he opened his own business as a TV and radio technician. Our mother supported all his decisions and they had complete trust that God would help them persevere. Our father would tell us this story and always close with, "God was very good to us, and we never stopped praying for help, that is why I owe Him so much."

The author and 3 of her siblings in front of the early house where Ignacio first opened his TV and Radio repair business.

Our father loved mathematics and his love of reading was evident by all the reading he did on a daily basis. He read every page and article in the newspaper to be involved in his community, politics, and any news that affected him or his family's future. He subscribed to Catholic newspapers and periodicals and he would read those too, cover to cover. He enjoyed listening to several radio shows including sport events. He had a Jewish friend who owned an electronic supply house whom he enjoyed discussing philosophical, political, and religious subjects with. He loved to discuss the Jewish beliefs and customs with this friend. He would sometimes share his friend's viewpoint on faith with us at the dinner table. He was an avid learner, and at age 76 he learned to operate a word processor in order to type his sermons.

I remember him listening or watching Billy Graham on television. When pressed for answers as to why he was so interested, his response was, "Billy Graham is a servant of God and we need to respect what he is saying. He has a message for all of us," Never mind that Billy Graham was not Catholic. I know some Catholics did not agree with his sermons, but our father took great interest in Mr. Graham's messages. Even politics turned out to be a good subject for him and his friend to discuss. They would compare the economy against the Great Depression and tried to predict the future of money markets. He said they both shared a love of their faith, and both were extremely religious. These occasions when our father stopped at his friend's supply house were some of the happiest moments of his day.

Our father had once commented to me that while he was at Kelly Air Force base as a supervisor, his subordinates and some other workers would ridicule him for being a devout Catholic. Our father would walk away from off color jokes or stories where people were unfaithful to their wives. He did not tolerate vulgar conversations or vulgar language. Our father was very respectful with everyone and expected respect in return. He knew he had to make a move where he could surround himself with good Christian men. After he began his own business, this was no longer a problem.

He joined the Holy Name Society at Immaculate Conception church and started attending retreats. He eventually became its leader and its president. He then became a St. Vincent de Paul Society member and its president for several years. His file drawers included information on over 800 families that he had assisted throughout his years as its president. He eventually established a small food pantry at the church and kept it stocked. He would sometimes get a call from families who needed food or would hear a knock on the door of his home from people needing food. He would get up immediately, even if he was eating his dinner, and go assist them. Our mother sometimes suggested he finish his dinner before leaving but he could not eat while others were starving. At times, inebriated people would knock at his door and he would take the opportunity to minister to them and invite them to Sunday Mass. He still helped them but not at the level he would assist a family. If he saw them at Sunday Mass, then he would register them with his block captains for food assistance. He never ran anyone away from his home without helping in some way, even if it was just listening.

Ignacio (front row, far left) with other church leaders and
volunteers and Fr Albert Storm around 1956.

His parish was a poor parish and so the need for assistance was great. He established block captains in the neighborhood for the purpose of the distribution of food. These block captains assisted him with distributing food in their particular areas and kept our father informed about the neediest folks in their respective areas. Only God could have created such a spiritual servant like our father. It is hard to believe why some people still question whether God is here among us. This organization served the poor with donations from the Food Bank of San Antonio, and if the parish had money our father would assist them with monetary help for utilities or medical needs.

Chapter 6

Starting His Own Business

⟋⟍⟋

Our father placed his sign advertising his TV and Radio Repair business in front of our home in 1955. This neighborhood now knew he was in business and since they knew him from church, he received many calls. He did his own bookkeeping and our mother helped him answer phone calls. On weekends and some weeknights, she would accompany him on his service calls just to get out of the house. Our father would get lost on some streets, but when our mother rode with him he arrived to his destinations easily. He admitted he had a bit of a problem with his sense of direction. He had to rely on map books for locating streets in order to make his calls. San Antonio was a new city and it was growing due to its military presence. It seemed like every year he had to buy a new map book because of new street names registered in San Antonio. His business did not interfere with his attending the 6:00 am Mass daily, and sometimes when he had to attend Holy Hour[10] he closed his shop early.

---

[10] Holy Hour: A long term tradition in the church of spending an hour in Eucharistic adoration in the presence of the Blessed Sacrament.

Ignacio and Catalina in the TV repair shop.

These service calls would get our mother out of the house and displayed to us his desire to spend some time with her. During these service calls, they talked about their day and the pressing concerns of each child that needed immediate attention. As children, we would tag along and sit in the station wagon watching our father until he disappeared into the homes, and sometimes we met the customers too. We enjoyed eavesdropping into our parents' conversations because it was always about one of us. We either were in trouble or had mastered a subject in school. After these service calls, our father stopped at a drugstore near his shop to buy us ice cream cones. The owner of the drugstore always greeted us with a smile and was amused as we ran out of the station wagon into his store. We handed him a nickel and received an ice cream cone in return. What a treat that was for us kids.

The first station wagon I recall riding in did not have windows besides the rear, front, driver, and passenger windows. We would bound into the station wagon and away we would go making our Sunday family visits. Our trips would begin after attending Mass and after we had eaten our lunch. Our parents did not allow us to ask our aunts or uncles for anything to eat or drink because they too had financial burdens like our parents and were raising large families. If we needed anything like the use of the bathroom, we were to approach our mother first, then politely ask our aunts for their permission. During one particular visit, I remember skating on a sidewalk, falling, and striking my thigh under a metal cyclone fence. I cut my thigh with a deep thick gash. I was too frightened to tell my parents so it healed on its own, but it obviously needed stitches. My cousins and I handled the clean-up and kept playing. I did not feel the need to interrupt my parents while they were visiting my aunt and uncle. It was not something we were allowed to do unless it was an emergency.

Our mother patiently waited for our father to finish his day before she heated up his dinner. She mastered the role of a supportive and loving wife. Her face shined with joy when our father walked into the house after a long day, and we too were excited to see his smiling face. She truly was a

Christian wife and mother, so full of energy for all of us. She loved to sing at Mass and as I mentioned earlier, had a knack for whistling. Sometimes, when I close my eyes I can hear her singing and whistling and imagine her in the kitchen preparing dinner. I love that scene; it was a happy time for me.

She was her own critic when it came to cooking. She stated that the only reason she cooked was to feed everybody. She felt her cooking was not anything special but we felt otherwise. She loved to prepare vegetables. Every kind of vegetable she could find she prepared. It is because of her that we like vegetables so much. When a poor family prepares a meal it is usually void of vegetables. Our mother made sure that did not happen in our home. One of our aunts still lived in Sabinal and her family picked vegetables for farm owners. If our cousins were traveling to San Antonio, they would often bring us a huge supply of whatever vegetables were in season. We did not have the pleasure of eating at restaurants like other families, but our mother tried her best to introduce us to all kinds of foods, except fish. She did not care for fish but during Lent and on Fridays, she prepared some kind of fish. She did not deny us the foods she did not like. She was considerate that way.

Our father's parish priest, Fr. Albert Storm, did not approve of our father leaving his job at Kelly Air Force base. He tried to convince our father into staying at his civil service job. But our father had already received his divine guidance from God, and he knew God would help him and our mother in this new venture. He had already prayed for discernment from God and our mother seemed to understand his point of view. Our father knew that starting his own business was the right move for him and his family. Our grandfather passed away in 1955, not long after our father had moved him into our home. I cannot imagine a pregnant woman with five young children caring for a cancer stricken tall lanky man all by herself. This act of love by our mother was a tremendous job for anyone, but especially for this small framed pregnant woman. Our father was very appreciative to our mother for her sacrifice of caring for his father. He often shared this story with us giving our mother so much credit for her heroic acts of care, especially in this particular situation.

My mother was small in stature but huge in generosity toward others. She loved our grandfather like a father and wept when he passed away. She did not express love for her faith as easily as our father did, and at first upon meeting her she was reserved and shy. She was "a Mary and a Martha[11]" rolled into one person. Our father's eldest sister called her a "servant" of God and never stopped thanking our mother for her service to our grandfather. Her example of caring for our grandfather had a profound effect on me and on everyone who had the pleasure of knowing her. She loved unconditionally and never boasted or asked for recognition. She went about her business of helping others silently and without much need for attention. She stated that God was in charge, and He was the one dictating how she would live her life. That's when I knew our mother was also given a gift of service much like our father. God gave her many graces during these hard times to persevere through what came before her.

Their marriage was a perfect match of two Christian people who loved and obeyed God's laws toward all fellow man. The bonus was marrying and seeing God's plan unfold for them in very special ways. They were a beautiful couple that complimented each other's natural gifts from the Holy Spirit. They displayed unconditional selfless love toward others and this was an amazing example to us all. It was as if God had touched both of them at the same time and drove them towards each other. They were in perfect tandem loving, caring, and respecting immediate family, relatives, and God's people. Their faith became a topic of conversation with everyone, not because they brought it up, but because their advice always included God's love.

---

[11] Mary and Martha : In Luke's gospel Jesus visits the home of Mary and Martha who are sisters, Mary sits and listens reverently to Jesus while Martha tries to make sure everything is just right in the home for his visit.

Our mother joined a Christian mothers' group, the Madres Cristianas. They met once a month to pray for all families in our parish and for families all over the world. She was an amazing woman whose love penetrated into the toughest hearts and earned her the position of "favorite aunt" to many of our cousins. She had the courage to speak the truth to our cousins who relied on her for advice. This was a loving gesture on her part never thinking of whether she would be accepted or rejected. She was clear in her messages and delivered them with love.

Catalina (front row, 2nd from the left) with the Madres Cristianas and Father Steuben in 1954.

Our parents believed wholeheartedly that their rewards were in heaven. Our mother lived humbly all her life almost in the shadow of our father. Our mother was strong-willed and she persevered as she had promised to our father in caring for others, especially our grandfather. I do not know about the nature of his stomach cancer, but I can imagine she must have worked tirelessly to care for him. She fulfilled this duty with much care and unrestrained service to our grandfather. I recall those awful spoonfuls of tonic we had to endure every week. This tonic increased our iron content and was an ensurance against childhood illness that affects many poorly nourished children. Her days were full of housework and endless chores. We were always a priority before any household chore or housework.

Our parents believed that God had full confidence in their ability to parent making them committed to family first. She would often say that becoming an orphan at an early age was a blessing because it forced her to become independent. She felt her teen years as an orphan had prepared her for the "hard life" she and our father experienced. We often asked her how she managed the house, children, our father, and our grandfather during those difficult and demanding times. She always gave us the same answer, "by the grace of God." Her favorite words of advice to us, "if you have your health, you have everything."

Our mother stayed home to care for us even though our fathers' income was not enough to sustain all our needs. Our father worked long hours to ensure he could pay for our Catholic education. He had the important task of reviewing our grades and our report cards. If the grades were not to his liking, he would have a little wrinkle on his forehead. He did not say much but this silence was "loud" enough for us to "hear" what he was thinking. However, if they were good grades, then it was time to congratulate us happily over the dinner table. He would pay off his credit line at department stores where we purchased our school uniforms and shoes just in time to start a new school year. Charge accounts from large department stores were the only way he could afford to dress us in school uniforms and shoes. We were not like other families who saved for vacations or holiday travel. Our money was for our Catholic school education because it is the most important education we received in our formative years. Our parents considered family their first ministry and knew God had empowered them to raise us to the best of their ability in the Catholic Church.

Our mother did not drive, so she was dependent on our father or the bus service to take her to places like shopping or doctor appointments. Our mandatory vaccinations needed for school came at a reduced cost from a neighborhood clinic established for the poor and uninsured. If vaccinations were not available at this neighborhood clinic, we would go to a clinic supported by our aunts' convent, the Missionary Servants of St. Anthony, where we received injections at a low cost. This nun was so nice and she recited the Hail Mary every time she injected the needle into our arm. She said our Blessed Mother would make sure the shot did not hurt. Sr. Anthony was so sweet she even reserved a lollipop for us. We dreaded those trips because we knew as we approached the clinic there was an injection in store for us. I believe that little nun lived to the ripe old age of 90 or so. God rewarded her with a long life.

The Catholic schools our older siblings attended were located in different parts of the city. The Catholic high schools were expensive, but our father had complete trust in God that his business would sustain these expenses. Since we were walking to school, which was a block away from our home, our father was free to drive our older siblings to school until one of them was old enough to drive. Sometimes they would carpool with their friends. Our father purchased used cars for us as we began to work and save money. The idea that we were growing up and getting summer jobs to help defray the costs of our education made our father happy. As a family, it was important to unite in this goal of completing our Catholic education. He stated that someday we would be proud to say we contributed to the cost of our Catholic education. The neighborhood Catholic school was very convenient for us until it closed its doors in 1968. It was time to find another Catholic school that accepted elementary, middle school, and high school students. We found that school on the south side of San Antonio, St Teresa's Academy. It was also the home of the Teresian sisters, where one of our aunts, Sr. Lilia, was a member. Her community of sisters lived above the school, so we saw our aunt very often.

Our parents offered a temporary home to many extended family members who wanted to move to San Antonio. A noble act easily accomplished by these two generous people. It was as if they were the same person. Our parents had experienced poverty and discrimination in their early days as a family, so they felt great empathy towards others who were still living in that environment. Our parents disciplined themselves to accept God's will in all things. I do not recall our mother complaining about their assistance to family members who wished to settle in San Antonio. I remember that one of my father's aunts, his mother's sister Paula, whom he was close to became very ill. She must have been in her nineties because I remember as a ten-year-old child that she looked very old.

Our parents converted their living room into a bedroom for her. The small town she lived in, Sabinal, did not offer the medical care she needed. She had some kind of illness that killed her outer skin cells at a very rapid pace. I witnessed our mother sweeping and mopping our wood floors constantly cleaning behind our aunt. Her skin was literally coming off her body shedding dead skin cells everywhere she went. We all shared one bathroom and I recall our father asking our mother to disinfect the bathroom immediately after our aunt exited. That was a tough job for our mother because she had eight children to care for too.

Our mother saw herself as a "servant of God". I now say as our father did of his mother- **my mother was a saint**. It did not matter that this woman was not my mother's aunt, just that she was in need. She passed away not long after she left our home for the hospital.

Our parents, humble as always, never discussed their generous gesture towards our Great Aunt Paula to anyone. I know God was pleased with our parents. He was watching their every move and gave them strength and perseverance to help when called upon. I vaguely remember her husband, our Great Uncle Thainis, came with her and he too stayed at our home, but in a different part of the house. Our mother was responsible for their meals and their laundry. These elderly folks were poor and did not have much so we gladly shared whatever we had with them. They did not have children of their own, but they did raise a niece of theirs, Anita, after her father, our Uncle Celso, had passed away. After their death, this niece and our parents became very close. Our father would speak to us about them, often admiring them for living in a segregated town all their lives and suffering through great humiliation.

Chapter 7

Corporal Works of Mercy[12]

~~~

W hen one of our father's sisters, Lilia, entered the Teresian Sisters
convent at 17 years of age with the full permission of our grandparents, the Order sent her to Cuba as a missionary even though our aunt
had only an eighth grade education. Our grandfather's hope was that the
Order would educate her. She was the eldest of our father's sisters and the
first one to join a religious order. In the late 1950s and early 1960s, Fidel
Castro stated that he never believed in God even though his parents baptized him in the Catholic Church. He suppressed Catholic institutions in
Cuba and considered himself an atheist. I do not have the complete story
of why our aunt was in danger, but it must have been a terrible situation as
our father became very concerned for her safety.

Our father petitioned the Teresian Sisters to find a way to get her back
from Cuba. He revealed to us that this was a very fearful time for our
family. He had to contact government officials because her Order did not
receive assistance in their attempt to bring her back home. He kept himself
informed about the terrible happenings in Cuba. Finally, our family was
extremely happy to learn of our aunt's impending return from Cuba. Our

---

[12] Chapter title: Corporal Works of Mercy: These are actions that are taken to help others.
Some examples include feeding the hungry, providing shelter to those in need and visiting the sick.

father carried her out of the airplane when she arrived in the United States. He tells us she was so emaciated and weighed about 80 pounds or less. Our family felt great respect towards our father for this heroic act of working hard to bring our aunt home. He did not want recognition and simply said, "I asked God to help me and he kept His promise, I owe Him so much for answering my prayers." It was not until Pope John Paul II made a visit to Cuba in 1998 that Fidel Castro brought back the celebration of Christmas to his country. Our aunt loved our father so very much and was always praying for our family and for our parents. They shared a huge love for each other and she would phone our parents every week as a matter of courtesy.

I mentioned our grandfather had hoped our aunt would receive an education since she was only 17 years old when she joined the convent, but it was not to be. They did not educate her, nor did they teach her to speak English. After her arrival from Cuba, she became a housekeeper for the nuns instead of attending school. She was the most humble person I have ever met, much like our father. Our father was very disappointed our aunt's order did not provide her with an education. We really did not have the reason why they did not educate her. Perhaps it was bigotry or poverty that was keeping her down. Our family agrees that she was one of the holiest and saintly individuals we have ever known. We can attest to her devotion to God and her complete surrender to His work in the Catholic Church.

My younger brother and sisters and I were very fortunate to have attended a school owned by the Teresian order. We saw our aunt on a daily basis and admired her incredible devotion to her service at the convent and school. Her tasks were many and not of much importance because it was labor, but she completed them faithfully and joyfully. I was elected student council president in my senior year in high school. My teachers shared this with our aunt and it gave her great joy to see me succeed. The school nominated and elected me Ms. STA (Ms. Saint Teresa Academy), an honor bestowed to a student who best represented their school. It had to be a person who excelled in school and displayed a love for others in many forms, especially service. Our parents were escorted to the third row of our auditorium and sat close enough to the stage to see me receive this honor. I was surprised and wondered why the nuns kept asking me what I was planning on wearing the night of the awards. I also was surprised to see the nuns making a fuss over my parents when they arrived at the auditorium. Our parents rarely attended any of our functions due to their busy lives with our family and our father's business, so it was nice to see them there. My parents were proud of me and thanked the nuns for the honor. Our father was so very pleased and turned to me and said, "I know you are happy, but I am joyful." It was nice to see someone from a poor family receive such an honor.

My Aunt Lilia accepted her Order's duties with love and joy and praised God for her life of service. She passed away in December of 2004, a few months after our mother passed. She loved our mother very much because our mother took care of her father and her little brother with great personal sacrifice. Our mother passed away on September 29, 2004. Our mother was a guardian angel to many due to her unrestrained service to many. She passed on the feast day of the Archangels. Her funeral was on October 1, 2004, the feast day of St. Theresa, the Little Flower. I interpreted this as a sign from God that our mother passed on to her eternal reward with the help of her guardian angels and St. Theresa. Since our aunt belonged to the Teresian nuns, I hoped this meant both women were together enjoying their eternal reward alongside of St. Theresa.

One of our uncles, Telesforo Simon, passed away from medical complications due to injuries suffered during the Korean war. Three other uncles returned from the war safely and married. Our father loved his brothers very much and prayed for their safe return from the war. He named all four of my brothers after our uncles. Uncle Telesforo Simon spent a few years at a psychiatric ward in a Veterans hospital in Waco, Texas due to the tremendous mental damage he suffered while a prisoner of war. He spent many years at a VA hospital due to these problems until his release in the early

1970s. Upon our uncles release from the VA hospital, he asked our father if he could live with us. Our mother and father gladly received him as part of our immediate family. We loved him like a brother. He just integrated into our family and became one of us. He too attended daily Mass like our father beginning his day by consecrating himself to God.

Ignacio visiting his brother Telesforo in Waco, TX some time in the 1960s

He was a quiet person by nature, but I imagine his years as a prisoner of war made him even more withdrawn. When our father was pressed for answers regarding our uncle's captivity, he stated that he would never share what our uncle experienced as a prisoner of war. Our father felt it would affect and change our view of our uncle. He did not want us to feel any pity, sadness, or to be too compassionate towards our uncle. He had been a soldier and we were to respect that great sacrifice he made for the safety of our country. Our uncle received the Silver Star and the Purple Heart for his service in the military.

Later, our father secured a lease at a nearby home for our uncle. We saw him every day and our mother became his caregiver. She did all his housekeeping, laundry, and prepared his meals. Our father would deliver his breakfast, lunch, and dinner to check up on him. Our uncle and our mother shopped on the same day of the week at the same grocery store. This way if he had any questions at the grocery store, our mother would help him. When they had finished their grocery shopping, one of us would drive them back home. One time when uncle was home convalescing from surgery, he handed me a grocery list of items he needed from the grocery store. On the reverse side of the paper, he wrote the exact location of where these items were located. This drawing looked like an architectural drawing of the store. It was as if he had taken an engineer's rendition of the store and drawn a blueprint of the store with groceries located all over the store. He had a photographic memory and was very intelligent. He would thank us repeatedly for any little thing we did for him.

My Uncle Telesforo was a very special person and we cried when he passed away. Our father often worried that he would pass away before our uncle. Our father did not want anyone else, especially us, to be responsible for our uncle's care. Our father had made a promise to be his caregiver and wanted nothing more than to care for him personally until his death. Our uncle's passing was painful for our father, but he knew this was what he had prayed for. Our father cried loudly when our uncle passed. We had never heard our father cry before that day. His heart was broken and yet it was filled with gratitude to God. Not long before our uncle passed, he had to have a leg amputated at the knee due to an infection he had suffered on his right foot. He had a prosthetic leg but preferred his wheelchair. His days of attending Mass and shopping were very limited. Our father would bring him Holy Communion daily and would make sure all his needs were met.

Our uncle was about 5'9" with a medium build and was a little more muscular than our father was. He had an infectious smile like our father and was always grateful for the smallest favor. They resembled each other very much, not only in physical appearance but in love for God. Their habit of expressing gratitude to God for all His blessings was a tremendous lesson for us all. We learned a great deal from watching them. As we would unload his groceries from our vehicle, he would thank us over and over. He was a handsome man who probably would have made a great father, but it was not to be. One would think that a man who suffered as a prisoner of war would become bitter, sad, or angry. However, with our uncle the opposite was true. He loved everyone and was a happy and content person. God gave him the grace to persevere and to live happily with us. Our father thanked God every day that his little brother had survived the war and was with us to love. I guess we shed tears when he passed because we considered him a brother more than an uncle.

Our father made sure we stayed in contact with extended family as often as possible, so we made car trips on Sundays to visit relatives. We would pack up and take the long drive to Waco from San Antonio during the time our Uncle Telesforo was at the VA hospital. Our father also had a brother, Uncle Frank, who lived about 1.5 hours from San Antonio, in Uvalde, Texas, whom we visited too. He also had a large family and we loved visiting and playing with our cousins. He was younger than our father, however, he passed away before our father. He resembled our father so much that when our father entered the funeral home for our Uncle Frank's Rosary[13], our cousins ran to hug him tearfully telling him how much he reminded them of their dad.

---

[13] Rosary: This service is a long tradition that is usually held the evening before the Funeral Mass. Family and friends and others paying their respects gather, usually at the funeral home, to pray and remember their loved one and includes the recitation of the Rosary prayers.

We would also visit our aunts at their respective convents. As a child, I did not understand how fortunate we were to have religious members in our family. Our father reminded us that they were always praying for our family's intentions. These women devoted their lives to prayer and to God's service. This was a beautiful expression of their love for God. By this time, we had a station wagon with windows throughout and we were always excited to ride with our parents. Our mother's family consisted of seven sisters and one brother. Her brother, Francisco Campos' was the favorite in their family and our mother loved him very much. Uncle Franciso lived in California, and he visited about once a year. One of his sons, Frank Jr., did not want to move away and stayed behind to live with us as a member of our family. We treated him like a brother. Our aunts, uncles, and cousins held our parents in high esteem due to their unfailing service to others. Frank Jr. continued to visit our mother almost weekly until her passing.

Chapter 8

Educating the Children

~~~

God helped our parents send all ten of their children to Catholic schools. This expense was a personal sacrifice for our parents, foregoing vacations, personal luxuries, and a larger home in a better neighborhood. At one time our father was offered a very good deal on a home in a more prestigious neighborhood. However, our father declined stating the expense would not allow us to attend Catholic schools. Our education was more important than having a prestigious place to live.

Our mother was one of eight children born in Mexico. She and her siblings eventually left Mexico for the United States where they settled in the small town where our parents met. She wanted to go to school but their impoverished situation was such that she had to work with our grandmother, Maria, as a housekeeper to provide food and shelter. Her mother was involved in a car accident that took her life shortly after they moved to the United States. Our mother stated that her mother and her friends were riding in the bed of a pickup truck, and were racing another truck loaded with boys when the driver lost control. Our grandmother fell out of the vehicle as it rolled to a stop. When they approached her, she drew her last breath and died. Her mother, my grandmother, was the only person killed. This left our mother and her teenage sisters orphaned in a small, segregated town in Texas with no one to rely on. This was another hardship for our mother that prepared her for the life she was to have with our father. Three of the girls and her brother had married and moved away to places where they could find employment.

Later, our father encouraged our mother to attend evening English classes offered at our parish, Immaculate Conception. It was within walking distance for her and she invited some neighbors to come as well. She succeeded in learning to speak some English and became a citizen of the United States. She taught herself how to read and write in English. She loved to read the birth, wedding, and funeral announcements in the newspaper. Since Spanish was her native language, she was a master at reading and writing in Spanish. Our mother assisted our neighbors who were illiterate in their letter writings to their families. She would read them their letters and then they would dictate their responses to our mother as she wrote. As a child, I found this interesting and did not understand the immense service our mother was performing. As children, we did not understand why our mother was doing the writing as they were dictating. The neighbors were very gracious and appreciative of our mother. It wasn't until I got older that I admired our mother for what she was doing for these families who had no one to help but our mother.

Her language of preference at home was Spanish. She ensured that we did not forget our Spanish. Our father felt being bilingual was an important skill to master for our future. Our mother was an organized individual and had a routine to her day. Sometimes poverty causes people to give up on dreams and depress people into feeling helpless, but not our mother. She envisioned her children becoming educated, having their own families, and prospering with grandchildren. Some individuals persevere at any cost or struggle. Only death can stop their drive for perfection and success. That was our mother. She had a drive to love her life and her children, and she accepted everything that came her way; her husband's illness, our grandfather's care, poverty, and even the death of her children. She loved completely and unconditionally everyone that needed her. Her faith in God and the prayer sessions she had with our father held us all together. One of her favorite sayings was, "Do what you can today, we do not know what tomorrow brings. Follow your first thought all the way through and trust God."

The family on Ignacio and Catalina's 25th wedding anniversary in 1965.

The Catholic elementary school we attended was on the Immaculate Conception Church site and it was within walking distance from our home. I learned to speak English and relied on my older siblings for help with homework. Our father was busy working long hours and came home rather late from his work. Our parents continually reminded us that good grades were all they expected from us. Getting along with our siblings was very important because we studied together and shared bedrooms. I have vague memories of living with my older siblings; however, they are the ones who remember the many relatives who made our home a temporary shelter. I have heard their stories of how our parents made room in our home for many of our relatives until they could find their own place. This house, although larger than the duplex we moved from, only had one bathroom. This must have been a lesson in patience, charity, and love for everyone who lived in our home.

Any time our parents talked about those difficult times, it seemed rather normal for them to provide shelter to extended family. The family members that lived with us visited our parents often up until their passing. Much like foster children, they would express their tremendous gratitude to our parents all through the years for giving them an opportunity to stay at our home. It was beautiful to see how our parents responded so humbly and without much fanfare. They did not want any recognition or thanks because they did things for others out of love and kindness. They loved others unconditionally and did everything asked of them by God with great joy and enthusiasm. Our father considered these opportunities of helping others as gifts from God. They found great joy in seeing others succeed as they did.

The struggles our parents experienced early in their marriage gave them the immense compassion they lived by every day. If we gave them a compliment for their kindness, they responded with, "Give God the credit. He made it possible." Nothing ever got in our father's way when it came to his service in the church or service to others in need. He was jubilant to serve God's people. He lived forever in gratitude to God for all His blessings. As a child, I loved to hear him tell jokes and laugh with us. From time to time, he found humor in some of our everyday situations. He loved to watch all sports, especially boxing and baseball. The younger children were not allowed to watch television past 8:00 p.m. Those shows were for adults only, besides our parents wanted us outside running around getting our exercise.

The first house on Hazel Street we rented did not have an indoor bathroom, and the outdoor bathroom did not have electricity. Our mother washed our clothes on a washboard since we did not own a washer or dryer. We eventually bought a washer for our home, but the dryer had to wait. The clotheslines were all our mother had to dry our clothing. I remember as a child, those winter months when it was very cold outside, our clothes would freeze on the clotheslines. We knew

washers and dryers were available, we just could not afford to buy them. One night our mother was bringing in laundry from the clothesline and one of her legs fell through a rotted board on the back porch. This demonstrates how old this house must have been. Our family lived in that home for about ten years before moving down the street into our new home.

Chapter 9

Buying the First and Only Home

~⌒

The story of how we acquired a larger home involves a very kind and observant woman. Our mother and some of us were walking from the bus and an elderly woman who lived down Hazel Street stopped us. This is what she said to our mother, "I have noticed your family keeps growing and I would like to sell you my home so that you can be more comfortable." That woman was a blessing and a miracle for our parents. God kept His promise to provide for our parents even in times of great financial stress. Our father met with her and was able to purchase the home at a very reasonable and affordable price. He eventually paid the home off and was elated to share that accomplishment with us. Always giving God the praise and thanksgiving for allowing us to have a home of our own that we could share with others who were in need of help.

Our mother enjoyed sharing a funny story regarding the move. One of the relatives put our baby brother crib in the back of their pickup and moved it with him still in the crib. I think our mother took joy in sharing that story with us because it reminded her of the many nephews and nieces who helped with the packing and the move.

Our mother was pregnant at the time of the move to our new home. The baby she was carrying stopped moving one day while she was working during the move. Our mother once again had the excruciating pain of burying another baby. As we grew older and began to understand our mother's pain, she revealed to us how she regretted not taking better care of herself during that particular pregnancy. She blamed herself for working too much during the move. Sadness and sorrow consumed our mother once again. We could not afford a funeral, so our father borrowed magnetic signs from a funeral home to place on the doors of his station wagon, using it as a hearse. Only the older siblings accompanied our father to the cemetery for the baby's burial. I believe our mother was still convalescing at home. I was five years old at that time and I remember our mother being sad and in bed for a while. Our sweet mother blamed herself, and for years she found it difficult to forgive herself. They baptized her at the hospital and our parents decided she would share our mother's name, Catalina Norma. Her burial was at a Catholic cemetery in San Antonio, San Fernando #2. Not long before our mother passed, some of our siblings bought a beautiful marker for our sister's grave and revisited the grave with our mother. God gave her a memory that day of her little baby girl and reminded her of that particular time. That was a blessing to see. For with God, nothing is impossible.

Our new home was much larger than the duplex with a larger yard. I had heard the neighborhood was once a Belgian plantation and that the smaller homes in the neighborhood served as homes for the workers that worked the fields. The woman who sold us our home was an African American widow and she bought the home from her employers. The home had wooden floors, a long hallway, high ceilings, transom windows and a large yard. It also had two large bedrooms, a dining area, a kitchen, a long hallway and a living area. It had enough room for our growing family and we loved having a large backyard. We doubled up in the bedrooms with two beds, some bunk beds, and made the dining room into a bedroom for portable rollaway beds. The house had a screened in porch, which was sometimes used as sleeping quarters if we had an overflow of guests. This porch eventually became a laundry room with a washer and dryer. The old garage the house came with had an old broken-down piano in it and an adjoining shed. We used to play with that piano until it was removed because the garage and the shed were falling apart.

A back-alley street behind our house was used as a shortcut by the neighbors to the adjoining streets. This alley had homes that resembled small worker's homes used at one time by field hands. There were one or two African American families living on our street. They were owners of homes purchased from plantation owners who left or passed away. Our father tells us that quite possibly the woman who sold us our home may have experienced some of the days of those plantations. Our neighbor, Mr. Green, was also African American and quite elderly, but he loved to toss pomegranates over the fence to us kids. His yard had a large pomegranate bush we loved to eat from.

Our father developed bleeding ulcers in his early thirties. Seeing him ill was sad and extremely strange to us children. He had at least three episodes that affected him so much that he was bedridden for a few weeks. Having our school within walking distance was a blessing. It was difficult to see our father in pajamas during the day and watching him with a diet of baby food and soft foods. He ate this way for a year to allow his stomach to heal from the ulcers. According to our father, his physician, Dr. Pedro Miniel; suggested he start some kind of hobby to distract him from the pressures of his responsibilities. It was hard work to carry the financial uncertainties of a business and of raising a large family. Our father took his advice and decided to plant pecan trees in our backyard. We had two pecan trees in the yard when we moved there. He made it his mission to heal and take some time for himself. We enjoyed many years of pecans and even learned to store them in sacks. The raking of the leaves during the winter months gave us all something in common to do. From the youngest to the oldest sibling, raking leaves was everyone's responsibility. To this day, I remember our parents stating that caring for these trees saved our father's life. They provided shade too and when we all gathered it was nice to sit with our parents underneath these big shade trees.

Our father had some of the existing pecan trees grafted. The pecans were too small to my father's liking, so he ordered the grafting of branches from trees with larger pecans. The tree surgeon came over and worked on our pecan trees. I remember seeing the trees' "wounds" from the newly attached branches covered by some type of fabric. He was also treating webworms, as pecan trees tend to attract them. We found this extremely educational and fun. It gave us all a project and a distraction from everyday life. He paid us five cents a tree to fill the moats he dug around the trees with water. These trees allowed us to spend time with our father asking questions and we made this a family project. Our brothers pruned these trees every year, as some branches began to grow over the roof of our house. The trees grew older and eventually stopped giving fruit but the memories of picking pecans was always fresh in our minds.

As we grew older and graduated from high school into college, our father could see the success of his sacrifices as we became first generation Americans with a college education. This education was from Catholic schools and nothing made him prouder than to see us graduate. Our graduation photos hung on the wall behind his desk. This way he could show all his friends who visited his home his "pride and joys" as he called us. He knew moving to San Antonio proved to be the best decision he ever made. He reminded us that without God all our accomplishments would not have been possible. Thanks largely to our mother's agreement to make our education their only goal in life. Our father believed consecrating oneself to God at the start of every day and his daily Mass attendance made all of life's hard choices easier and he received many blessings.

Our mother told us that even in times when our father's business thrived, he remained humble. These qualities made our father very approachable and easy to talk with. He thanked God during daily Mass for any business coming his way. He promised God that he would never forget the poor or allow his business to take priority over his commitments to God. He continued his work with St. Vincent de Paul Society distributing food to the needy. Our father knew God had kept His promise of helping him raise his ten children in the Catholic faith. He was a conscientious business owner and he charged very little to those who could not afford to pay him. He did not work for free but his compassion and understanding of families that struggled with finances had a place in his heart.

His business was successful because it provided for his family's education. Our parents never took vacations, time off, or spent money on anything considered a luxury. They lived for, and only for, their children. They prepared us for life by educating us and instilling in us the faith they had in God. I have seen families divorce or give up when facing hard times. In our parents' case, struggles were a bonding event for the family. Our parents fought for their happiness and they persevered. I am sure there are other successful families who may have experienced these same struggles as our parents, however, I feel what makes our parents unique is all the care our parents provided to others in addition to raising such a large family. Our father never lost faith in God even during the rough times when our father was too ill to work; he depended on God's blessings to heal him. Without his faith in God, he would say, "I would not be here today." Our father never tired of telling us how much he owed all his successes to God. God had kept his promise to help our father during the good and the bad times of his life. For this reason, he would ask us to start every day with a Mass or by consecrating ourselves to God for His guidance and protection.

In 1974, the Archbishop of San Antonio, Patrick Flores, invited our father to become a Permanent Deacon[14] in the Catholic Church. Our father was greatly humbled and prayed for discernment. This was a big decision for our father because our mother had to be in complete agreement to share our father with the Catholic Church and the people of God. She lovingly agreed and our father began attending classes at Assumption Seminary for

---

[14] The duties of a Permanent Deacon are in three broad and essential functions: the proclamation of the Gospel, the service of the liturgy, and the administration of charitable works in the parish and community.

5 years in preparation toward becoming a Permanent Deacon. Our father was humbled to receive this honor, yet he could not contain his enthusiasm for the Seminary classes. He would close his shop early on those days of class, shower, eat an early dinner, and away he would go. Sometimes, while he ate his dinner he would express such love for what they were learning in class. His dream of serving God that he had since he was a young boy had come true. He was very thankful for this privilege and honor to serve God as a Permanent Deacon in the Catholic Church.

Ignacio in an undated picture probably in the early 1970s

He revealed to us that if he had not met our mother, he would have become a priest. Our father felt this was a calling from God and he was going to make this opportunity as a Deacon a priority in his life. After his ordination, he semi-retired from his TV repair business and devoted more time to helping at the local parish. Eventually, he cancelled his shop lease at 1531 S. Brazos and moved his business home. This would save him rent money and would keep him available for God's people. His attendance in daily Mass when the Archbishop was at our parish, and subsequently when Fr. David Garcia and then subsequently Fr. Bill Collins were the assigned pastors, helped to solidify their relationship and the Archbishop understood our father was a man of God. The Archbishop himself was Hispanic and a member of a large family, and he marveled at how well our father managed his large family and still made time for Mass, assisting the poor, and now working towards becoming a Permanent Deacon. Our father would humbly respond that God was at the forefront of everything he did and that he had complete surrender and utmost trust in God's promises.

As children, our father would prepare breakfast for us after attending Mass and before driving us to school. He would sometimes comment that he was the only one, besides the celebrant, in attendance at some of the morning Masses. He would often comment that if people knew how much grace they would receive from daily Mass, there would be a greater attendance. We had daily Mass at our school, so we did not accompany our father to the 6:00 a.m. Mass. Our father made it his personal promise to God to serve the poor, the marginalized, the unwanted, and those in this humble parish, Immaculate Conception, that he had lived in for over 45 years. His daily Mass attendance gave him the grace to continue his promise to God to serve others to best of his ability until his death. He felt he could not do enough to repay God for all the mercy God had shown our father by blessing him with a healthy family, an educated family, and a vocation he always wanted and life itself.

Our father always stated that his faith in God came from his devoted mother, our grandmother, Mariana. God gave him the grace to persevere in circumstances that seemed impossible to escape throughout his life. According to our father, she was a "saint." She was a prayerful person, attended daily Mass, suffered great poverty, but most of all she offered all these sacrifices to God. She credited her survival from poverty to God, as did our father. Our father accepted human suffering with joy and stated that all good things follow a period of suffering. He was a testimony that God never forgets us. He sometimes would tell us stories of how God had answered his prayers during a troubled and hopeless time. He shared some of these stories in some of his sermons too. He would prepare his sermons with real examples of God's love for him. These personal stories were very heartfelt, and our father somehow found a story for every sermon that fit the readings for the day so perfectly. This inspiration for such sermons could have only come from the Holy Spirit. It was an absolute delight to hear his sermons. He preached and practiced what he said. We enjoyed listening to him and seeing how well he incorporated the gospel messages into his real life experiences. God kept His promise as a caregiver for our father and our family.

Chapter 10

Our Father is Ordained as a Permanent Deacon

~~~~~~~~

Our father was ordained a Permanent Deacon on December 17, 1979, at a lovely ceremony at Immaculate Conception Church. It was a new beginning for all of us. We would now have to share our father with the church, but more important we would be witnesses to what he had always wanted to do; serve God every day. He was humbled by the invitation to join the Deaconate program and at peace to serve God in this capacity. We were all almost adults then and were starting to have our own families. When we would attend Mass at his parish when our father served Mass sometimes we would stay to help him lock the church. He gave sermons straight from his heart that related to the gospel message of the day. During all the years as he was raising his family, he was active in our parish. He was in charge of the St. Vincent de Paul Society as its chairperson for many years. Only because no one else wanted the responsibility and he felt the importance of this ministry. It seemed like he was president throughout all the years he served.

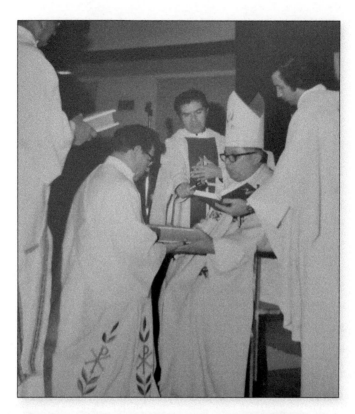

Pictures from Ignacio's ordination as a permanent Deacon.

He was the "go to" person for food or clothing needed by the poor of his neighborhood. These people did not need to be Catholic to receive assistance. However, our father took every opportunity he could to tell everyone about the graces one receives by attending Mass and living as a child of God. The church also established a fund to assist folks with their utility bill payments. However, to qualify for assistance our father had some questions he was required to ask before issuing a payment. He had to complete all the information that was asked in these small cards he submitted to the St. Vincent de Paul organization. This encounter gave him an opportunity to minister too. He loved working with the poor of the parish, and it seemed like there was always an emergency he had to respond to at the church. Our parish Pastor at that time, Fr. Bill Collins, did not have a pastoral associate so our father occupied that position as well. He felt he was living his life just as God was asking him to do.

Our mother was very patient during the time he was away with his duties as a Deacon. He served at countless funerals and accompanied the families to the burials. He gave baptism instructions to the parishioners, taught religious education to engaged couples, and married many, including our siblings and me. He was the most selfless, loving, caring, and accepting person one can imagine. This man who had been on his deathbed three times, was doing so many things in God's name that people marveled over his dedication to his ministry. Our mother was just as generous since she had to share him and his time away from home. She understood his mission and she was patient. She truly was the ideal wife for our father. She was selfless, honest, and supportive.

Our father had natural leadership abilities and was a humble man, always careful not to appear arrogant about anything. He was probably the happiest during these years of doing God's work. He also recited this statement in response to questions regarding this steadfast service to others, "I owe so much to God because he has blessed me with so much." He was indebted to God for saving his life in times of great illness. He also was grateful for all the business that came his way during hard economic times making it possible to provide a Catholic education to all his children.

Our mother stayed home, and she too had a loving heart for others and their struggles with illiteracy and poverty. She enjoyed visiting the elderly. She made time for friendships even though she had such a large family. Our mother was always ready to be a counselor to those who needed guidance. She joined church groups and she made sure we faithfully attended Mass on Sundays and Holy days of obligation. During the month of May, as children my sisters and I would offer flowers to the Blessed Mother after attending the 6:00 p.m. evening Mass. We would process into the church dressed in our First Communion dresses and veils holding bouquets of flowers. After Mass, the Rosary and the Litany of the Blessed Virgin Mary[15] were recited

---

[15] Litany of the Blessed Virgin Mary: Is often prayed as part of the Rosary as a devotion to atone for sins and pray to avert calamities.

as we delivered our flowers to our Blessed Mother. Our brothers served as altar servers and helped our father as needed.

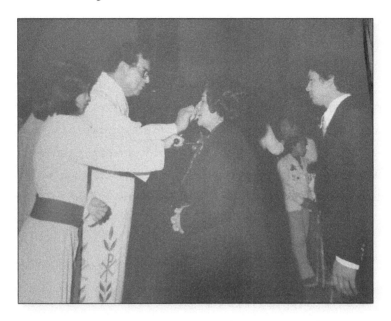

More from the day of Ignacio's Ordination; giving Communion to Catalina and the family that day.

As we walked to church, the neighbors who did not have children would cut flowers from their gardens and hand them to us. By the time we arrived at the Church, our small bouquet of a few flowers grew to a beautiful bundle of flowers of all kinds. Our mother loved flowers, and every year she planted annual flowers and they would bloom colorfully under her care. She loved flowers and we delighted in bringing her flowers during special occasions. Our mother was very dedicated to the Blessed Mother, especially after her own mother passed away. She made sure we prayed the Rosary as a family during the month of May. We would kneel in a circle in the living room and take turns praying the decades of the Rosary. As we grew older and our responsibilities increased, it became difficult to get everyone together at the same time. However, that did not stop our parents from praying their Rosary. They were dedicated to Our Lady of Guadalupe.

Without question, community service was a way of life in our home. We spent our weekends helping people assigned to us by our parents. Our mother volunteered us to help clean the convent in our local parish. We helped in many ways like house cleaning, printing music flyers, or just sorting papers. My younger sister and I also accompanied a nun and a priest to the "missionary" places located at the outskirts of San Antonio to give Holy Eucharist, Confirmation, and Confession preparations. As teen-agers, we took turns driving an elderly nun, Madre Antonia, to her doctor appointments twice a month. During this particular errand, our mother would accompany us to help. She did not want Madre Antonia, who was elderly, to struggle in and out of our car. She did not speak English so our mother's ability to translate back and forth kept Madre Antonia and her doctor engaged and kept the visits effective.

Our mother instilled service in our lives by sending us to our friends' or relatives' homes that she considered overworked or overburdened to help with household chores. Our mother had many friends, and it was imme-diately apparent that she had much empathy for those with large families. One of my younger sisters and I would spend Saturdays with some of these folks helping with household chores. We did not refuse or argue with our mother when she made a request for our help. Our father would drive us, and I can only imagine what a sacrifice it was for him to leave work to perform this work of charity. He worked on Saturdays, and we usually needed his rides in the morning and then in the afternoon when we were ready to come home. I still wonder how our father managed being the only driver in our family for so many years. As our parents would say, "God keeps His promises, we just have to ask."

Once we started driving, these community services became more frequent. Our brothers were helping our parents around the house or at our father's place of business at 1531 S. Brazos. As we became of working age, we would secure summer jobs to help defray the cost of our education. I do not remember spending that money on luxuries like other kids would. We were responsible and contributed to the family expenses that seemed never ending. Our father paid for all of our medical costs without the benefit of health insurance, except for the insurance coverage offered by the school during the school year. He was grateful that hospitals and doctors back then accepted monthly payments for their services. Life seemed much easier back then, but I am sure for my parents it was a blur as they struggled to educate us.

As we matured and started our own families, our husbands and wives enjoyed our large family gatherings, and everyone contributed with jokes and funny story telling. Our children played together and shared dinners and playtime. Our father was a quiet man and loved being home because his job sometimes required a lot of driving. Our father was a homebody of sorts, so all of our celebrations were planned at their home in the event our father had to respond to a call regarding St. Vincent de Paul or a Church duty.

He loved being home with our mother and enjoying the peace of home. He enjoyed his pecan trees, his sports on television, and most of all his quiet times. Those were times for praying and asking God to protect his children. It was also a quiet time for sharing stories between him and our mother.

He enjoyed bringing greetings from the parishioners back to our mother that always put a smile on her face. They would reminiscence about the "old days" and the friends they had left behind in the small town where they had met. He enjoyed having his grandchildren around him and he enjoyed sharing their stories and their dreams for the future. Our mother was very loving, she loved children, and she saw helping out with the grandchildren as serving God. She took care of some of the grandchildren, and she did it with such joy and happiness. Like any family, we celebrated births, high school graduations, weddings, and other holiday events. Soon the grandchildren were attending college and moving away. It seemed like time was passing by so fast.

The family was growing with new births and our parents spoke about looking forward to their time in heaven. Our parents grew older but we never noticed the changes they were going through. Seeing someone as often as we saw them made it difficult to see the aging process. They always had a smile for us. Our mother loved to ride with us to stores for shopping or on visits to our homes. Being the ever helpful person she was, the first thing she did when she entered our home was ask if she could help out with housekeeping or projects we had begun. She had an energy that was envied by all of us. She loved to help out and if she could lighten our workload at home, since we all worked outside the home, she would. These works of charity came automatic to her and she would be offended if we did not respond with love and kindness.

She loved plants and flowering plants were her favorite. She wanted to know all about the flowers and their blooming cycles. It was a joy to see her face when discovering new flowering plants. She loved working in her garden and she actually preferred working in the yard over housecleaning. Whenever I see flowering plants I always think of her and the joy flowers brought to her.

Our father continued his responsibilities as a Deacon and he never tired of helping or serving others. He did all this with a smile and for the love of God. He was repaying a debt to God for his many blessings. He felt he could never repay God for His help in the education of his children, and for his health after being very sick most of his life. Our father continually reminded us that "God keeps his promises." A problem was never as big as we felt it was because our father would calm us with stories of the miracles that God granted him and our mother. He always offered reassurance and prayer. He requested that we surrender completely and totally to God in all things.

Parish priests frequented our home as well as retired priests who befriended our parents. Our father loved their visits and their conversations. I think our father felt camaraderie with them. These friends, who happened to be priests, understood our parents' sacrifices of raising large families in the Catholic faith. These friendships expressed great respect towards our father and mother, and our parents were humbled by it. Our mother made them feel at home and one particular priest, Fr. Frank Gomez, called them Dad and Mom. Fr. David Meurer visited them weekly and loved to tell jokes and hear my dad's stories. He passed away 4 months before my Dad.

Catalina and Ignacio with Archbishop Flores the year of their trip
to the Basilica of Our Lady of Guadalupe in Mexico City.

Our parents were invited by Archbishop Flores to accompany him to the Basilica of Our Lady of Guadalupe in Mexico City, Mexico. One of my older sisters and her husband gifted our parents with tickets for their trip. Our parents accepted the tickets and our father joined a group of Deacons who were invited to serve Mass at the Basilica with the Archbishop. God kept His promise of being our father's caregiver by bringing him great joy in the privilege of serving Mass at the Basilica. Our parents felt humbled by this honor and talked about it for a long time. My sister made them very happy and it was an event that was hard to forget. All was blissful and beautiful. Our Lady of Guadalupe was our father's favorite image of the Blessed Mother. He had great faith in her and her miracles. He gave his second daughter Guadalupe as a middle name. A large painting of Our Lady of Guadalupe hung on the wall behind their bed; a reminder to pray the Rosary in thanksgiving for the many blessings credited to the Blessed Mother's intercession.

Chapter 11

50th Wedding Anniversary

~⌒

I t was 1990 and we began to discuss celebrating our parents' 50th wedding anniversary with them. We all agreed that we needed to make this a beautiful celebration of their 50 years of life together. We planned to invite all their friends and relatives. The planning for the anniversary celebration in April of 1990 for our parents involved all of us working together. Father David Garcia expressed great joy in celebrating this event with our parents, since they were so humble yet generous. He stated that our father and mother were indeed a rare couple who placed all their trust in God by serving others and deserved a great celebration of life.

One pleasant surprise of that celebration was a visit from one of our uncles, Blas Martínez, who lived in New York, and whom our father had not seen since the 1940s. He was invited to our parents' celebration, however, we were not aware he was actually coming to Texas since we had not heard either way. He just showed up during Mass during the "kiss of Peace[16]" and approached our parents. Our father recognized him immediately and they embraced. Uncle Blas had settled in New York after his service in the military and did not return to Texas. The story of his return was instigated by divine intervention as well. The miracle of our uncle's return to Texas

---

[16] Kiss of Peace or Sign of Peace: during the Catholic Mass the congregation asks for peace and unity and greets each other with that same wish for all.

was a direct result of his son's dream drawing him back to Texas to find his roots.

At the 50th Anniversary reception with his brother Blas (on the right) who they hadn't seen since the 1940s and his brother Franciso and sister Sr Lilia.

One night, our cousin, Blas' son, had a dream that he was at a cemetery looking for his grandparents' tombstone, and when he woke he shared this story with his father. He then booked a trip to Texas to find those tombstones and to visit all of the many cousins he had never met. Coincidentally, we were planning our parents' 50th wedding anniversary celebration, so he convinced his father to come. This cousin was in his thirties before he met us, his cousins from Texas, and he eventually made Texas his home. He now lives outside of San Antonio and has moved his father back to Texas.

Our father was admitted into Santa Rosa hospital the day before the 50th wedding anniversary celebration. He had spent the day preparing the church for Mass when he suddenly felt dizzy and began to perspire profusely. He waited in the pews until his dizziness passed and cautiously drove home. It was only two blocks back to our home from his church. As he drove up the driveway, he hit his car horn to attract attention. I was at my parents' home visiting when I heard the horn. I ran out to the car and our father was complaining of dizzy spells and nausea. I forced him to move over and to allow me to drive him to the hospital. Our mother followed later and rode with one of our siblings to the hospital. The doctor hospitalized him and ordered a few tests to find the cause of his dizziness. No alarms were sounded for a heart condition or problem, he just seemed tired.

We spoke to the physician who reassured us that our father was likely suffering from exhaustion, and probably just needed some hydration and rest. Our father was a diabetic and admitted consuming sweet bread that was loaded with sugar that day. In addition, he led a very busy schedule at the church and he rarely rested during the day. He also admitted to eating oranges, and that prompted the physicians to gravitate towards a diabetic incident. Our father was a good patient and took all his medications as prescribed. His physician had suggested that perhaps it was my father's high blood sugar that may have initially caused the dizziness. However, we now know it was the beginning of his heart failures and not just effects from high blood sugar.

The next morning, we pleaded with the physicians to release him since he was feeling better after spending the night at the hospital. He came home in time for the 50th anniversary celebration. Our father was excited to be going home and seemed to be feeling like a new man. Full of excitement for their 50th wedding anniversary party, he wanted to see all his family together in one place. The evening was perfect and he did not suffer any health problems. I should qualify that statement; he did not seem to have any more incidents after this first episode.

From the 50th Wedding Anniversary Mass and reception.

Today, I still wonder if we should have taken him back to Santa Rosa hospital for further testing. Would things have turned out differently? Unbeknownst to us this was a prelude of things to come. It was determined after his death that he probably began to have heart problems and that the dizziness was all part of the heart issue. The doctors said that having mini strokes during his sleep was also possible. Our father continued to have a few episodes of dizziness and did not give it much attention. Had he confided in us perhaps we would have helped him get the proper care he needed. He would tolerate the dizziness until he felt better and then go on his way. I remember one time, he was sitting in his bedroom and I stepped in to say hello. He revealed to me that these dizzy spells seemed to be more frequent but that his doctor thought it was due to his diabetes. His symptoms were masked as a diabetic problem, however, we discovered after his passing that they were much more serious. He had massive clots in the arteries surrounding his heart. I accompanied my father to one doctor appointment in which his doctor checked his carotid arteries. Some slowness and clogging was present according to his checkup, but it was nothing to worry about. However, he was not referred to a cardiologist or a vascular specialist at that time. His primary physician was ready to retire at 70+ years of age and our father trusted him. I did not realize that our father's condition merited further study from cardiologists and vascular doctors. Perhaps a second opinion from another physician could have helped avert his heart attack.

Our father was very dedicated and never put his own personal needs before his duties as a Deacon or with St. Vincent de Paul. After our father's death, we spoke about the heart condition warning signs he had experienced. Still, we felt regret because we did not recognize the heart disease symptoms. I can now see God's plans unfolding as I relive this story. God had a plan for our father, and he was preparing him to go home. Our father had expressed to us on many, many occasions that he "just wanted his bell to ring." He wanted to leave this earth quickly and without much trouble for anyone, especially his children. He was very excited to be close to death and finally rest in God's hands.

Over the years our mother's health began to deteriorate and she seemed a bit more delicate than our father. Her pains came from her diabetes, with all its complications, in addition to high blood pressure and congestive heart failure. However, the most serious concern was the progression of her dementia. She was growing increasingly irritated because she could not remember some simple everyday events. We were witnessing our mother becoming increasingly frustrated with her forgetfulness. Even her facial expressions displayed annoyance with her confusion. We did not know that this was an advanced case of dementia. Nor did we see how serious this condition was interfering with her everyday life, her brain was failing slowly. We did not observe her behavior as too serious but as part of the aging process. It wasn't that we did not care for her, it was that our visits were always about us not her.

We visited our parents' home almost daily, a haven of encouragement, love, and a good meal. Our father continued his ministry and charity work, and by now began to show signs of slowing down too. Our mother asked him to retire from being an active Deacon but he would not hear of it. This work was God's work. Again, at this time, it appeared our mother had the larger health issues and she was the one that needed our full attention. Our father's focus always seemed to be our mother and her health. Never once did our father mention his continuing dizziness and bouts of profuse perspirations, as if he purposely wanted to steer our focus away from him.

Chapter 12

60th Anniversary and the Millennium

~~~~

In the year 2000, we began to talk about celebrating their 60th wedding anniversary knowing full well that they would not agree to any kind of a huge celebration. They considered the 50th anniversary celebration too expensive and they reminded us that they were simple people. We agreed that they were right, so we scaled down to a family Mass. The immediate family had now grown to 20 adults and 32 grandchildren. We were involved with our day-to-day lives and raising our own children. Our father was noticing the decline in his own health and our mother's, and we could see his concern in his eyes when he spoke about her. He was responsible for her doctors' visits and for refilling and distributing her medications. He would worry about her whenever she was home alone. She had been leaving the gas stove on and walking away to take care of other things. One evening she left the water running all night after she had watered her plants and the neighbor came by early the next morning to turn the water off. She was easily distracted from moment to moment, and this created a dangerous situation for her and our father. He began to share his concern about our mother with us a little at a time. I suppose he did not want us to feel burdened, just informed.

However, as time went on we noticed our mother's dementia was affecting her more and more. At the same time, our father seemed "older", slower, and seemed like he was beginning to show more concern over our mother's safety. He worried more about her than his own health. However, we could see the "tiredness" in his face and we encouraged him to retire from the church, but he did not agree. He was indeed a faithful servant of God who knew no limits. This tremendous faith in God can only be explained by the many graces he received throughout his life by serving others.

He surrendered his trips to the San Antonio Food Bank location to a younger driver whom he sent to make the food collection runs for the parish's St. Vincent de Paul food pantry. He still unloaded, inventoried, and distributed the food, he just could not make the drive to the Food Bank anymore. He did not trust himself driving because he was concerned about his health and those dizzy spells. He mentioned that he did not want to drive very far from the neighborhood. When he had to drive to funeral homes at night to lead a Rosary for someone who had passed away, he would ask one of us to drive him. We seemed to discount these as signs of aging and nothing more. He mentioned he was going to do God's work as long as he was capable and able to find someone to drive him to where he was needed.

I suggested we celebrate our parents' 60th wedding anniversary with a brunch at the Fair Oaks Ranch Country Club after a Mass of thanksgiving to God for their long lives as a married couple. I suggested that we all create a gift for our mother and father made by our own hands. We settled on a quilt for our mother made of twelve squares representing her twelve babies. Each one of us created a small fabric square with some representation of our family. We had each square sewed into a quilt for our mother. We designed two extra squares with crosses on them for our two siblings that had passed away. Because there were twelve squares, the pattern was a perfect square and her quilt turned out beautiful. We placed this quilt in her casket when she passed as she had asked. She was a sentimental lady even though her toughness was the first characteristic many noticed when meeting her.

The author speaking at the reception for Ignacio and
Catalina's 60th anniversary celebration.

The idea of something for our father's desk or his wall in his office was suggested. We each wrote a letter or poem thanking our parents for all they had done for each one of us. Each letter shared our personal and unique experiences of growing up at their home and we shared some touching stories too. We each read our own personal letter to our parents beginning with the eldest on to the youngest. We then handed the letters to them already framed for our father's wall. The tears that flowed from our parent's eyes were tears of joy, they received the letters of gratitude with such humility.

Thanking them was simple but they would not take any credit for anything. At the bottom of each family letter every member of the family signed their name. The reading of these letters by our siblings and me to our parents was my favorite part of the celebration, besides the Mass. The grandchildren entered the church in a procession holding a flower designating love which was placed in a large vase in front of the altar. Then our parents entered with us behind them and took their seats. The Mass was a total surprise for the parishioners, and many enjoyed seeing our large family. The anniversary celebration was held in May of 2000. This was the year God chose to take our father, the millennium year, also the Great Jubilee[17] of the Catholic Church. Just seven months after the anniversary celebration, God would take our father home to rest.

Our father made a short speech stating that it had been an honor for our Mother and he to be our parents. He spent some time talking about his and our mother's faith in God. He touched on some of the struggles we all had experienced and yet he knew that prayer had sustained us during those dark days. He alluded to the rough start he and our mother had at the beginning of their marriage. He believed that God always kept His promises, so he surrendered totally to God's will. He explained why he recited the Rosary every day after dinner. He knew our Blessed Mother was smiling as he thanked God for another day of love and joy. He also explained that by walking up and down our sidewalk praying his Rosary, he felt that one of us would follow his example. He spoke about his dedication to Our Lady of Guadalupe through his Rosary since he was a young boy.

He reminded us to turn to God during good times and bad times. He believed that God never abandons us. He expressed that he had lived his life fulfilling his duty as a caregiver of God's gifts to him and our mother. He felt his "job" on earth was finished and that God was calling him home. He had raised and educated his children (gifts from God) to the best of his ability. He was ready to die, and he admitted he had prayed for a quick death. He did not want us to suffer with him or to have to care for him. He felt he did not want to burden any of us with long term care. He stated he

---

[17] Great Jubilee: The Great Jubilee in 2000 was a major event in the Roman Catholic Church, held from Christmas Eve (December 24) 1999 to Epiphany (January 6) 2001. Like other previous Jubilee years, it was a celebration of the mercy of God and forgiveness of sins.

was greatly humbled by these letters and that he would read them every day over and over. We all cried at that point.

Shortly after the celebration, he cleaned out his desk, organized all the church files and returned them to the parish. He began to have meetings with one of our brothers, Simon (the executor of his will), and gave him all the details of what he wanted in the event of his death. He was preparing our mother too, but she was not hearing it. She felt they would live a few more years. Our father was still driving to Mass, serving Mass, and continued his duties as a Deacon, all the while asking God to show him how to care for our mother's medical needs. He had passed the St. Vincent de Paul duties to other members of the church. He was serious about preparing for his death. He was so happy to know that death was close. He always talked about living in eternity with God. It was as if God Himself had conversations with our father about his death and the preparations needed for this transition to occur.

It was a beautiful Sunday afternoon on December 10, 2000, I was eating at a restaurant with my husband, Steven, and our two children Lucas and Adam. My husband's grandparents, Robert and Louise Benfer, were there too. The phone rang and I heard, "father is in the emergency room, he is not feeling well." "He is asking for you." It felt like a bomb had exploded in my heart. I panicked and asked my husband to rush me to Santa Rosa hospital. We left the children with his grandparents at the restaurant. When I arrived at the hospital, all my siblings were there. I looked at our father and hugged him. He said, "I am ok, I just felt a bit dizzy, these cardiologists are putting a stent in one of my arteries and I will be ok." I did not feel he was in any danger of dying, I was just bewildered about the whole thing. It all seemed too quick for me to absorb. I do not remember exactly how I felt but I do remember saying, "He looks strong and healthy." I was concerned but I never thought a simple procedure would take his life.

He expressed concern for our mother since he knew her dementia was progressing. He asked for my younger sister and asked her to care for our mother and her medical needs. She gave him the reassurance he needed as he walked away with his doctors to begin a simple, everyday procedure that happens thousands of times in every hospital. It was supposed to be simple, and our father was supposed to be alert after a day. These procedures are now an outpatient procedure and patients usually go home the same day. Some risks were mentioned as a formality but again all interventions into the body have some risk. There was nothing to worry about and the cardiologists stated our father was in good physical health for an 85-year-old gentleman.

As soon as the doctors said we could see him, everyone managed to see him. My sister and I were the last ones to enter the room to see him, since we had planned to stay the night at the hospital. I leaned in to say hello, and he pulled me close and kissed my forehead. I felt an immediate fear that he was saying goodbye. My sister teased him and asked him to kiss her too. He was fidgeting with his hands, so I asked him if he needed a Rosary in his hand. He shook his head in a positive way, so we began praying the Rosary with him and he stayed awake long enough to finish it.

After praying the Rosary, our father stared at the foot of the bed and made an interesting comment. He said, "Look, it's my older sister Juanita, I have not seen her in years." She had passed away many years earlier. Then he stared at the foot of the bed again. He looked very interested in what he was seeing. I asked him what he saw and he responded, "I do not understand what they are saying." This was the longest night of our lives as my sister and I discussed what we had witnessed. Sometimes when people are dying it is not unusual to hear them say that they see people who have passed before them.

One of our aunts, Sr. Rosemary, who managed the retirement center for priests (Padua Place) in San Antonio, was familiar with the medical procedure our father was having. She came to visit our father the next day and was upset that he was not fully conscious. He kept falling asleep and was not alert as expected. At first, the doctors stated it was because he was

85 years old, and that waking up from the anesthesia was difficult for some elderly patients. However, Sr. Rosemary stated that the anesthesia was not the problem and insisted that a neurologist exam him. After a few more tests, the doctors confirmed that something was seriously wrong, as our father was not responding to questions after two days. He stayed in the intensive care unit for about a week.

As the days progressed, he became combative and his responses to questions were confusing. He was moved to a regular room since his heart was functioning well, however, his mind was still confused and his breathing became labored. He was not able to eat so the hospital tried to feed him by inserting a tube into his nose. That tube malfunctioned and filled his lungs with fluid. His ability to walk or talk was failing. A CT scan was ordered and the tests confirmed that our father's brain was filling with blood due to a massive stroke caused by the release of blood clots during the stent procedure. It was a matter of a few hours before our father's brain would die. I was devastated upon hearing the news. Our mother was in shock and could not understand all the medical reasoning behind the negative prognosis and his impending death.

We began to prepare for his passing and discussed preparations for a funeral. It was a sad time for my siblings and I, but it was especially hard on our mother. She still hoped he would recover and go home to recuperate. She had been preparing his room and made sure she had everything he needed at hand, but it was not to be. He died at Santa Rosa Hospital on December 21, 2000, at 10:30 p.m. I can still see my brother, Simon, holding our father in his arms as he took his last breath. Our brother was reciting a prayer as our father's soul left his body. I know I should have felt relief that our father was no longer suffering, but I felt the opposite, I felt anguished. My oldest sister called our parish priest and our father's friend, the Archbishop, to give them the news. I should say joyful news but it did not feel like that at the time.

A few days before his heart attack, I woke up at 3:00 am from a deep sleep thinking about my father. I felt as if someone had purposely awoken me. I listened to a voice in my head asking me to reflect on my father. It said, "Why don't you write a letter to the Archbishop and tell him how wonderful and selfless your father is." So, I got up and wrote a rough draft of a letter. In this letter, I praised his charity work and his service as a Deacon. I wrote about his undying service to others throughout his lifetime. I also spoke of the wonderful parent he was. I mailed it and the Archbishop received it a couple of days later. The timeline in this is very interesting and I will try to explain it as I write.

The Archbishop's response to my letter was dated December 10, 2000, coincidentally the date of my father's heart attack and admission to the hospital. My husband Steven comforted me by saying that anyone dying in the year 2000, God chose for a special reward in heaven. I immediately felt a sense of peace. I was not expecting such a comment from him. It sounded correct as far as I was concerned. My father was a saint, and I knew he was greeted with a huge welcome into heaven.

My mind was filled with great sadness, despair, and disbelief, which all manifested into a depression. This was not supposed to happen. Whose fault was this? Did the doctors mess up? I was in a fog throughout the planning of my father's funeral. Our eldest sister kept replaying the visit she made to our parents' home the evening of the heart attack. She wondered if calling 911 for an ambulance would have saved our father's life. He waited in the emergency room for an hour before a doctor saw him. I suppose the staff thought he was having a diabetic attack or just maybe had a virus. Our father always downplayed his illnesses. I blamed myself for not accompanying him to his doctor visits to ask more questions regarding his dizziness. He had a habit of going to his appointments alone.

My mind could not accept his death. God knew my father was in the emergency room for one hour before he was helped. Did God plan this? Why didn't anyone see he was in need of assistance? What happened? I questioned the happenings of that day for a long time. I finally accepted that our father's passing was God's will. Our father told us almost every day he was ready to go, ready to die, and ready to begin his new life with God. Although painful to hear, these words expressed how much he welcomed death and spending eternity with God. He yearned for death. He knew our mother would be safe and that their ten children would care for her. He knew she would never be alone. He was confident leaving this earth with a content heart and a thankful heart for God who kept all His promises.

He looked so handsome in his coffin. He looked like a sleeping angel. He wore his best suit and his Deacon's stole. It felt just like a dream with everything going in slow motion. I was hoping to wake up to see that it was all a dream. My mind would not accept my father's death; it refused to. It was a difficult time and I stayed in a depression for months. I had to take leave from my employer. It all happened so quickly. However, eventually with Mass, prayer, and rest, I accepted his death.

Archbishop Flores came to see our father at the hospital and mentioned the letter he had received from me. His response came to me the following week dated December 10, 2000. What a blessing that his letter was dated the same day of my father's heart attack. It was a blessing from God. I imagine when the Archbishop prepared his words to respond to my letter he first prayed for our father. God does things in very mysterious ways and without any notice. I credit the Archbishop for praying for our father as God was preparing to take him home. Just 11 days later, our father passed away on December 21, 2000. The Archbishop's letter was dated December 10, 2000, a Sunday afternoon, the same afternoon our father suffered his heart attack. We thank God for that blessing from our Archbishop, one of our father's best friends who presided at his funeral.

Although I knew our father prepared all his life for his death, I could not have imagined a more painless death. Before all this happened, I often played a scene in my mind of caring for our father. I could see vividly in my mind's eye a family caring for their father as he aged and eventually passed away. However, that was my imagination working. God had other plans. I hear his voice in my mind every day giving me encouragement to keep going. I resemble my father, and people say I look like one of his sisters, Sr. Rosemary. She suffered from polio as a child and had to wear a brace on one leg. She ran around tirelessly in her wheelchair making sure her staff was always on top of things. If anyone missed our father just as much as we did, it was her. She often relied on his business advice when managing the convent and the nursing home. She was the little sister who lived with him and our mom a few years before she took her vows at the convent. They had a certain closeness and knew exactly how to read each other's hearts. She received her eternal reward to heaven in 2019.

I had 11 days to accept his illness and eventually his death. My mind would not accept his death and I fell into a deep depression. His death was literally a shock to my system. I did not know that depression can slip into a person's mind and overtake it. I was in shock during our father's Rosary and during the funeral. It was not until one week after his death that I "awoke" and found myself walking in circles in my home. I could not sleep, I could not control the high anxiety levels I was experiencing, and I could not sit still. I had heard others say that when a person loses joy it is considered depression. It's not just happiness we miss it's the joy that helps us survive every day that suddenly disappears. This is something not easily understood except through personal experience.

Chapter 13

Mom is Alone

~~

Taking care of our mother was very important to us. She had raised us all and provided a loving environment, and she deserved the same care in her old age. We all attended our first family meeting to discuss our mother's care and her medical needs. We made a unanimous decision that our mother should not be left alone at any time. The reasons were obvious; her age, her dementia, and of course our concern for her safety. This task of caring for her appeared overwhelming since we all had families and jobs. This meeting was all about discussing her needs as we perceived them to be. It was a first step in our mission to care for mother.

We decided that my sister and I would care for our mother during the day, and the remaining seven siblings would rotate spending each night with her. We had another sibling living in Dallas, and he did his best to visit often, usually on a weekend. Our father had designated our brother, Simon, as executor to his will and hence, he was responsible for taking over the finances and the business of running our mother's house. We brought or prepared meals for our mother during our shifts. At first, it was easy. She could eat anything we prepared. However, as time passed and her diet became restricted to certain foods, this was a difficult task. The foods she loved and had prepared all her life were off limits and so it was difficult to convince her to try new kinds of food, namely a diet best for someone with diabetes.

The experience of living without our father still felt unreal. Seeing our home with one parent absent was painful. Father was quiet but we missed him. Our mother had an abundance of medications prescribed to her by several doctors. Sorting out her medical needs and doctor appointments was an education. She would see four or five different doctors for a variety of illnesses. She herself was falling into a depression missing our father and not caring about her own health. It was such a chore just to get her to take her daily medications. I volunteered to drive her to her doctor appointments. I became familiar with her medical conditions and was able to follow up with the family through emails. I noticed that some of mother's medications had the same side effects. I had an opportunity to do the research when I noticed that her blood pressure was lowered to dangerous levels. When I brought this up to her primary physician, he decided to contact her other doctors and discuss her medication regime.

Our mother did not want to trouble anyone, so sometimes I had to be extra vigilant on what I perceived she was needing or experiencing. If she crinkled her forehead she was in pain. If she refused to eat and was sleeping a lot, that meant her sugar levels were off. These sugar levels were measured before and after meals. If she looked lost with far away looks, her dementia was roaring. At times, she would not have an appetite due to the side effects of these medications, making nighttime medications that required food intake a problem. She almost always stated that surely we must be poisoning her with so many pills. Taking medications is not as easy for the elderly. It is a task they do not look forward to simply because they have to swallow so many pills, usually three times a day. God was good to us, and we managed to pray for guidance to care for our mother. Our parish priest, Fr. Bill Collins, visited her often and his presence gave her solace.

After speaking with my husband, I decided to quit my job to care for our mother full time. I thought at the time that I knew nothing about caregiving. Oddly, I did not have to study or take a class or learn anything to care for her. It all came naturally. I made her my priority and then I adjusted my family life to hers. I fell in love with her all over again. I saw her decline into almost a "childlike" state before she died. I fell on my knees every day to pray for strength and patience during these last few years with her. I knew God would not let her suffer too much and that he was preparing a place for her. I am an optimistic person and I enjoy being happy, so these difficult times became a real struggle for me. I needed God to give me strength to see the positive side of my actions and to make my mother feel as special as she made me feel all my life. Sometimes, if I could, I would attend noon Mass at Immaculate Heart of Mary church because my mother's neighbor, Rosa, would come and sit with her while I went. The Mass gave me hope and peace during this difficult time.

Our mother lived in her own world, and we never knew if she fully understood what we were asking of her. At times she seemed lucid, but we knew she lived in a different reality because her eyes seemed far away. She did not participate in many conversations. It was as if she could not hear anything we were saying. It was sad to see our mother this way since she always had a sense of humor and was very friendly. Our mother loved her life and loved people. She wanted to live forever. One year, we gave her a baker's rack for her kitchen and she made the comment, "Too bad I am not going to live too long to enjoy it." The fact that her dementia robbed her of recognizing her demise seemed like a huge blessing. Sometimes she would say she wanted to die just because she was suffering so much. However, for the most part, she had no idea her life was ending. We continued taking her to Mass because she was able to sit and listen. We wanted her to receive Holy Eucharist and to experience God's healing.

Shortly after our father passed, she had a condition that required abdominal surgery. Her doctors delayed this surgery until it became absolutely necessary for her survival. After a year of suffering, she had surgery to correct rectal prolapse. It was a very serious surgery for anyone, but especially for an 85-year-old woman. We called Fr. Bill and he gave her a blessing before she went into surgery. An incision was made across her abdomen, and this meant lots of pain and a long recovery. I remember having to spoon feed her because she was refusing to eat due to her weakened state. Her will to live was weakening. She did not want to eat and she did not have an appetite. On many days she imagined that she had eaten when she had not. This was attributed to her dementia and slipping sense of reality. We wanted to help her gain weight, but it was easier said than done. She was so frail and helpless during this time and no longer the strong woman we remembered. It was during this time that she started to receive the Holy Eucharist from Eucharistic ministers that came to her home.

The days of raking leaves, pruning her rose bushes, and planting plants are fixed in my memory forever. She loved to move furniture around in our rooms from time to time. She claimed this would help us deal with changes that would be ever present in our lives. She was a classic home-maker, washing windows, changing curtains every season, gardening, and helping with church functions. It seemed like her work was never finished and she looked exhausted most of the time. She was such an impressive person with such drive to be the best mother and wife she could be. She became a sweet grandmother to all of our children. She enjoyed babysitting the grandkids and she found each one of them so interesting. She always tried to be an effective and efficient sitter for our children. She made them her priority. After her grandchildren were picked up and handed safely to their parents, then her chores at home began, and not before. Since she was such an amazing person who had struggles throughout her life, I often wondered where she gained such strength and perseverance. She relied on God to guide her and help her see these ten children grow up and become educated good stewards of the Catholic faith. Yet she was ready to help us with our children without any hesitation. She never retired from raising children or cooking meals for us until she became ill.

Every day I would leave our home at 7:30 am after dropping off my children at school, and arrive to bathe our mother and prepare her for the day. The sibling that spent the night with her did not get much sleep due to our mother's confusion between daytime and nighttime. Of course, mother would be tired in the morning and wanted to sleep. I would allow her a nap but mostly I would take her walking in air-conditioned areas for exercise. I did not want her to lose the ability to walk. I wanted to keep her legs strong. Usually, she would fall asleep in the car on the way to wherever we were going. My younger sister would help me care for her during the day, and sometimes when my sister was not with me; our mother requested a visit to her house, so off we went. Mother enjoyed that very much and usually we had lunch there.

Our family had just one income to rely on since I had left my job to care for our mother. My husband was not pleased that we had to budget, but love has no price. Gas was expensive in those days and my home was 30 miles away from hers in Boerne, TX. Sometimes after spending the night at our mother's home, I would go back and forth maybe twice a day. My children, Lucas at the time was 11 and Adam who was 8, had their father, my husband Steve, caring for them almost all the time since I was almost always with our mother. I am very grateful to my husband for his support and understanding. Prayer sustained me during the day and night. I never forgot my Rosary as our father had taught us to recite it daily. The Blessed Mother was guiding my every move and sustaining my love for my mother during these very difficult days.

The night duty person was responsible for mother's dinner. They could bring it with them, cook at home or even take her to their home for dinner. That was a nice break for me since I had prepared lunch and sometimes breakfast. This routine seemed perfect until our mother's health started getting worse. She began to lose her appetite, and this created a problem since her medications needed to be taken with food. In addition, her physicians began to recommend a diet specifically made for diabetic patients. It was not easy preparing her meals with foods she was not used to eating. The grocery shopping had to change to foods that were on her diabetic diet. Basically, almost everything in her refrigerator had to be relocated when her new diet began. We could not trust that she would stay away from these foods. Sometimes she hunted for food in the refrigerator, so we had to be careful with what we stored in the refrigerator.

One month after our father passed, we noticed that our mother was having problems with her stomach. She would complain about pains in her abdomen and she was in the bathroom for long periods of time. We noticed this and decided to take her to her doctor for an evaluation. Since her doctor had retired and a new doctor had taken his place, we decided that perhaps a gerontologist would be a better match for her. One of our sisters was familiar with a gerontologist and she made an appointment. He examined our mother and found that she had a problem brought about by her diabetes, rectal prolapse. He referred her to a surgeon for evaluation and it was decided that she needed to have surgery to correct this problem.

In February 2001, our mother had surgery to correct the rectal prolapse but remained depressed and confused. She continued her long periods of time in the bathroom, and this only aggravated her problem. There was a routine cleaning process that needed to be done every time she used the bathroom. This area was to be cleaned and medicated. This process was performed only by the women. Our brothers could no longer help us with our mother since her surgery. She suffered the entire four years with this condition, and it was heart wrenching watching her go through so much pain. After the major surgery a new problem arose, her heart was beating at a dangerously low rate. The focus was on keeping her alive with a healthy heart and strong lungs. She was suffering with congestive heart failure for a few years now; a condition that only got worse over time.

Sometimes she was exhausted and did not want to walk much. Her cardiologist recommended a pacemaker to help with regulating her heart rate. At the time our father was alive, she was being seen by a cardiologist who was always overbooked and kept us waiting sometimes an hour or more just to see him. So, we switched to someone recommended by our mother's gerontologist. This pacemaker was for regulating irregular heartbeats and it seemed like a good solution for mother. Her heart rate was in the 40s and she moved very slowly. One time while she was in our home, she "fainted" and her eyes rolled up in her head. I called 911 and when the paramedics arrived, they could not believe her pulse was as low as it was. The physicians decided to keep her in the cardiac ward in intensive care because her heart condition was worsening. Her breathing seemed labored and she struggled to walk more that two or three feet without gasping for air.

The pacemaker seemed the only solution to increase her heart rate, however, the procedure created a new problem. Just like our father, it caused a blood clot to loosen, and in this case it planted itself in her bowel. This started her road to her reward in heaven.

Two days after her pacemaker was implanted, my sister called me and said, "Mother has died. She was sitting on a chair, her eyes rolled back, and she stopped breathing. She does not have a pulse. José *(our oldest brother)* and I moved her to the bed in the chair and she opened her eyes and came to." I suggested they call 911 and take her to the hospital. When the ambulance arrived, our mother's pacemaker kept malfunctioning and her heart would stop and start. Our brother José rode with her in the ambulance to the hospital. The cardiologist at the emergency room at University Hospital called his class of students (it is a teaching hospital) to witness the mixed messages our mother's heart was giving the pacemaker making it trigger electrical impulses not needed by the heart. It was a malfunctioning heart and a malfunctioning pacemaker sending irregular messages. This was causing our mother's heart to stop and restart. He stated that this series of malfunctions was such a rare occurrence that this class may never see it again.

The physicians decided to keep our mother hospitalized for a short period of time. Upon her hospital release, she began having a terrible pain in her abdomen. I took her back to University Hospital and the doctors did not know what was causing the pain. It was not until the next day when the pain worsened that the doctors gave us the bad news. She had an obstruction in her bowel caused by a clot that escaped during the insertion of the pacemaker. The pain she was experiencing on her right side was due to the obstruction in her bowel. A colostomy was not an option due to her age, so her doctors voted against it. The physicians were now discussing surgery to try and alleviate her pain. Just as she was being wheeled into the surgery room our brother, Simon, and I arrived at the hospital. Our older siblings had agreed to allow our mother into surgery and were told that our mother would probably die in surgery. That was neither what we wanted nor what our father or mother wanted. Our mother wanted to die at home surrounded by her family.

God was present in that moment. The elevator opened and Simon and I landed at the very room where the surgeons were preparing for our mother's surgery. Our brother asked them to stop the surgery and asked how much time our mother had left. Was it enough time to take her home? Yes, it was, and we arranged to take her home the next day. We met with a hospice nurse and began to plan her funeral. Our mother was sedated due to the excruciating pain she was experiencing so we did not communicate with her very much. She was now on her way to fulfill the place God had prepared for her. I stayed with her the last night of her life and spoke in her ear telling her how much we loved her. Our eldest sister and her family prayed a Rosary by her bedside. I administered the morphine drops as prescribed by the physician during the night.

Chapter 14

Mom Goes to God

~

The next morning, we surrounded her with family, grandchildren, even neighbors who had such love for her. We called extended family members and they came to say their goodbyes. By this time, our mother had been in a coma for about a day or so. I spent the last night with her and I felt such a peace just being with her. She passed away the following morning on September 29, 2004, at 9:30 a.m. The last sounds she heard were family noise in the background. I have heard it said that hearing is the last sense to go, so we wanted her to hear us all having a good time. Just like when she would host us all in her home for holidays and parties. Our mother had the last rites administered to her on several occasions, and Fr. Bill Collins commented to me, "If she does not go to heaven, there is no hope for the rest of us." What a beautiful compliment he was paying to our mother.

Our mother's Rosary was held at the funeral home because we did not expect as many people in attendance like the crowd that came to our father's Rosary. To our surprise, the funeral home had standing room only and a line that extended outside of the funeral home. She was being honored for her service and her love of others just like our father was. It was a beautiful sight to see. God must have sent messengers to announce her departure because people came from all over Texas. Her funeral was held on October 1st and Archbishop Flores presided at her funeral Mass along with

Fr. David Garcia, Fr. Bill Collins, and Fr. Anthony Cummings. The church was full to capacity just like our father's funeral. Her funeral was held at Immaculate Conception church so that all the neighbors could attend. She was dressed in the white lace dress we purchased for the 50th wedding anniversary celebration.

My younger sister and I had taken our mother to a studio a few weeks before her passing to photograph her in preparation for her funeral photo. She wore that very same dress she was buried in. She had a fun time that day and I believe that was the last time she went out besides the hospital visits. She left a huge hole in our hearts when she passed. Many of the relatives she had given temporary shelter to made the trip to her funeral.

Our eldest brother, José, spoke at the Rosary about the many sacrifices our mother had made as a young mother raising ten children. He spoke about the many nights she waited for our father to finish his day to prepare his dinner. He spoke of her unending love for the poor and her dedication to our father. Her supportive love for our father when he was so ill was also a highlight of his speech. He spoke of her tremendous faith in God and love for the Rosary. Our mother lived for others and she was a shining example of a true servant of God. She never complained about our father's many commitments as a Deacon. She supported all his efforts in educating all their children in Catholic schools, foregoing luxuries and vacations.

Ignacio and Catalina on the 20th anniversary of his ordination to become a Deacon.

He spoke about her compassion for her neighbors who struggled with illiteracy, which deeply affected her. She made time to read their mail to them and to answer letters if needed. She was a wonderful grandmother full of patience and love for her grandchildren. She had a gleam in her eye for every grandchild. She loved to be a grandmother and she loved to see her grandchildren happy, especially when they arrived at her home. Our mother put others first before herself in every situation, whether for family or friends. She lived as a true servant of God and made it known how much she relied on His grace and mercy. She is forever in our hearts and I attempt to live as she did every day. We miss her very much but know she lived a full life together with our father just as God planned.

It has been over 2 decades since our father's passing and a few years less since our mother's passing. We miss them very much. As time is passing, I have noticed that our siblings and I do not visit as much as when our parents were alive. Our families are growing and we are becoming grandparents ourselves. That alone leaves little time for other activities. Some of us have retired and are traveling a bit around the world. The reality is that we are also aging. We have spoken on the telephone and emails regarding our common ailments inherited from our parents and have compared medications and treatment plans. Life is going by very fast now, but we are extremely grateful to God for our parents and their devotion to prayer. We appreciate our Catholic education and upbringing and strive to live as they did.

All of us have committed to service in the Catholic Church either by serving on committees or boards, joining a ministry, or just helping people in our parishes that need assistance. We know that spreading the Good News of Jesus Christ is part of who we are. We live by example to our children by thinking of God in all things and decisions. Life is continuing with all its struggles, but our faith is sustaining us just like it did for our parents.

We celebrate our parents' birthdays and anniversaries of their passing in our own way with our families and sometimes with each other. Our Catholic faith has carried us in good times and in bad times. We can only strive to be like our parents, totally committed to God in all that we do knowing God has our best interest in mind. He is our salvation.

The examples of love, service, and compassion that our parents have demonstrated to us will always guide our lives as we continue to be dedicated to God and continue to do His will.

Our father was a person who accepted his duty as a child of God by living every day of his life with compassion for others, personal sacrifice, love for the Mass, and love for family.

May Catalina and Ignacio live in eternal happiness as promised by God.

Author's Message

My intention in writing this book is to share my father's many acts of mercy and faith that helped him survive the obstacles that his life presented. He appreciated God's calling to serve the community. I also wanted to highlight my Mother's support of my Father's mission serving the community and as a Catholic Deacon.

Acknowledgements

Contributor: Lucas Daniel Hughes
Draft Feedback: Kenneth Rodriguez, Deacon Ray Jimenez
Editorial assistance: José R. Martínez, Jr.

Appendix

Family and friends from this story who have passed on to their eternal reward as of November, 2022. May they rest in peace.

Family
Deacon Ignacio Torres Martínez–my father
Catalina Campos Martínez–my mother

Rosario–their first baby who passed
Catalina Norma–their second baby who passed

Mariana Martínez (Ignacio's mother)
José Martínez (Ignacio's father)
Paula Torres (Ignacio's Aunt)
Juanita Martínez (Ignacio's sister)
Telesforo Simon Martínez (Ignacio's brother)
Francisco Martínez (Ignacio's brother)
Sr. Rosemary Martínez, MSSA (Ignacio's sister)
Sr. Lilia del Niño Jesús Martínez, STJ (Ignacio's sister)
Sr. Lelia Martínez, MCDP (Ignacio's sister)
Celso Martínez (Ignacio's brother)
Blas Martínez (Ignacio's brother)
Anita Martínez (Ignacio's niece)

Francisco Campos (Catalina's father)
Maria Campos (Catalina's mother)
Francisco Campos, Jr (Catalina's brother)
Juan 'Johnny' Luna (Catalina's nephew)

Friends

Madre Antonia

Robert and Louise Benfer

Fr. Bill Collins

Archbishop Patrick F. Flores

Mr. Green

Fr. Frank Gomez

Fr. David Meurer

Dr. Pedro Miniel

Rosa Ocejo

Fr. Albert Storm